François Quesnay

The Economical Table

(Tableau Économique)

THE OECONOMICAL TABLE,

AN ATTEMPT

TOWARDS

ASCERTAINING AND EXHIBITING THE SOURCE, PROGRESS, AND EMPLOYMENT OF RICHES,

WITH

EXPLANATIONS,

BY THE FRIEND OF MANKIND,

THE CELEBRATED

MARQUIS DE MIRABEAU.

TRANSLATED FROM THE FRENCH.

LONDON

Printed for W. OWEN, at *Homer's Head*, between the Two *Temple-Gates*, *Fleet-Street*.

M.DCC.LXVI.

François Quesnay

THE ECONOMICAL TABLE

[Tableau Économique]

BERGMAN PUBLISHERS

New York New York 10011

Published, 1968, by
BERGMAN PUBLISHERS
224 West Twentieth Street
New York, N.Y. 10011

First published:
London, 1766

Standard Book Number 87503-010-6

Library of Congress Card Number 66-28473

Printed in the United States of America

TO THE FARMERS OF ENGLAND,

THIS TRANSLATION,

UNDERTAKEN CHIEFLY WITH A VIEW
OF SETTING THE SUPERIOR USE AND
ADVANTAGES OF AGRICULTURE
TO THEIR COUNTRY IN A
CLEAR LIGHT,

AS THE ORIGINAL WAS TO PROVE THE
ABSOLUTE NECESSITY OF IT
TO FRANCE,

IS MOST RESPECTFULLY DEDICATED

BY THE TRANSLATOR.

PREFACE

BY THE

TRANSLATOR.

OF all the ſtudies purſued by mankind, hiſtory is generally allowed to be the moſt uſeful and entertaining, eſpecially that of internal commotions, as uſually diſplaying the greateſt exertion of the mental faculties. Yet what, after all, is even this branch of hiſtory, as handled by moſt writers, chiefly made up of, but the ſtruggles between knaves and madmen, followed by a diſciplined rabble of ſlaves and fools, for the wretched prerogative of trampling on the necks of their equals? How much more intereſting muſt be the relation and diſcuſſion of thoſe means, by which both nations and individuals may improve their happineſs, not only without interfering with each other's intereſts, but to the great and univerſal benefit of all. And this, indeed, ſeems, now at laſt, to be pretty much the ſenſe of the moſt thinking part of mankind, witneſs the good reception given to the works of BERKLEY, and ſome other modern writers on that ſubject, who have handled it with a profoundneſs becoming philoſophers, and a ſpirit worthy of citizens of the world.

BUT, with all their profoundneſs and ſpirit, it does not appear, that any of thoſe writers have, at leaſt demonſtratively, pointed out the primitive ſource of happineſs to ſtates, according to the nature, extent, and ſituation of their reſpective territories. For, though agriculture, manufactures, and commerce are, all, allowed to be highly uſeful, and the two former, particularly the firſt, abſolutely requiſite to the well-being of mankind in general, it has not, I think, been as yet demonſtrated, that they are not all equally objects of attention to every ſtate in particular. It has not been mathematically proved, that it would be

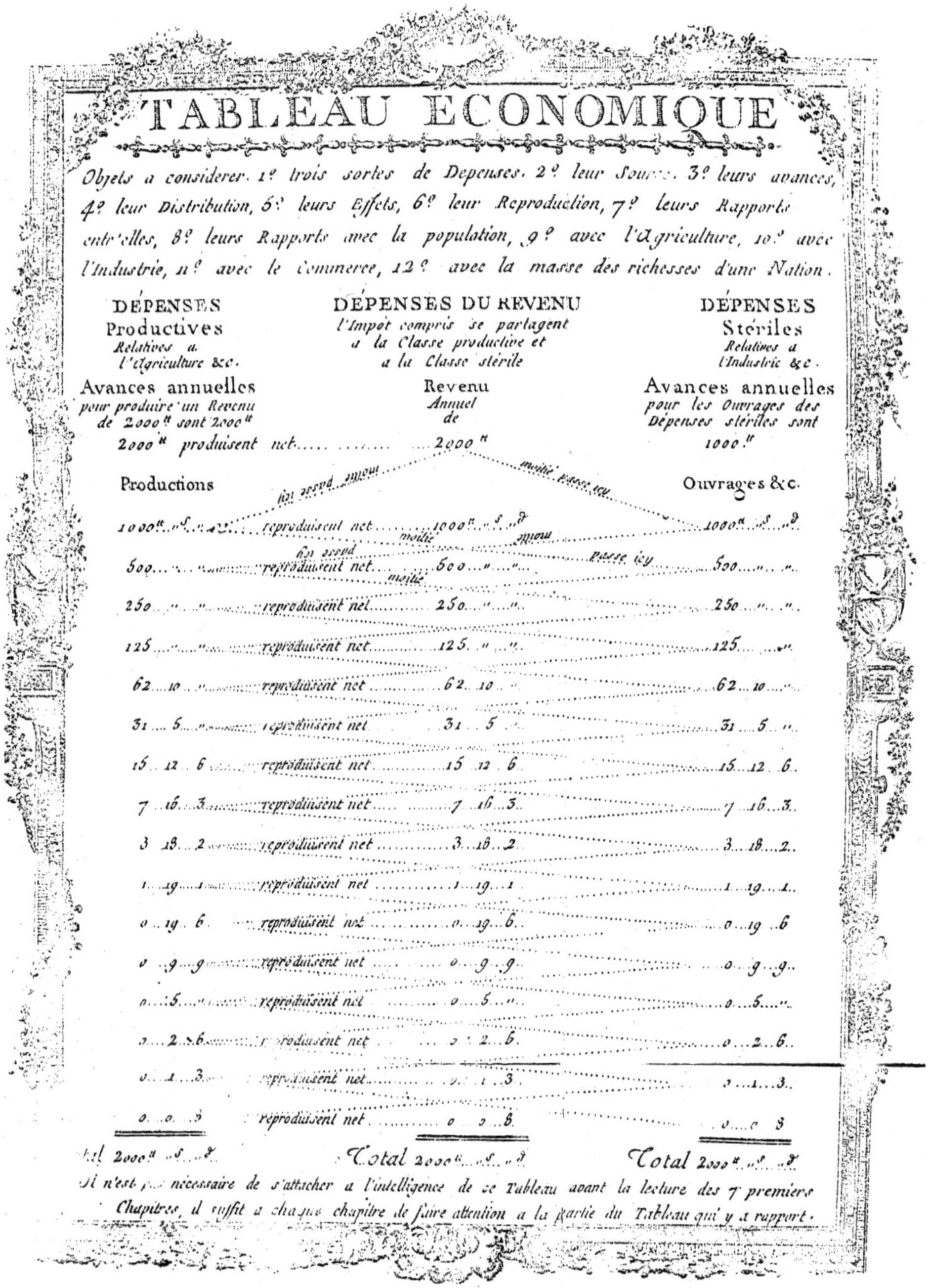

TABLEAU ECONOMIQUE

Objets a considerer. 1.º trois sortes de Depenses. 2.º leur Source. 3.º leurs avances, 4.º leur Distribution, 5.º leurs Effets, 6.º leur Reproduction, 7.º leurs Rapports entr'elles, 8.º leurs Rapports avec la population, 9.º avec l'Agriculture, 10.º avec l'Industrie, 11.º avec le Commerce, 12.º avec la masse des richesses d'une Nation.

DÉPENSES Productives Relatives a l'Agriculture &c.	DÉPENSES DU REVENU l'Impôt compris se partagent a la Classe productive et a la Classe stérile	DÉPENSES Stériles Relatives a l'Industrie &c.
Avances annuelles pour produire un Revenu de 2000.tt sont 2000.tt	Revenu Annuel de	Avances annuelles pour les Ouvrages des Dépenses stériles sont
2000.tt produisent net	2000.tt	1000.tt
Productions	moitié passe ici / moitié passe icy	Ouvrages &c.
1000.tt ..0 ..0 reproduisent net	1000.tt ..0 ..0	1000.tt ..0 ..0
500 ..0 ..0 reproduisent net	500 ..0 ..0	500 ..0 ..0
250 ..0 ..0 reproduisent net	250 ..0 ..0	250 ..0 ..0
125 ..0 ..0 reproduisent net	125 ..0 ..0	125 ..0 ..0
62 ..10 ..0 reproduisent net	62 ..10 ..0	62 ..10 ..0
31 ..5 ..0 reproduisent net	31 ..5 ..0	31 ..5 ..0
15 ..12 ..6 reproduisent net	15 ..12 ..6	15 ..12 ..6
7 ..16 ..3 reproduisent net	7 ..16 ..3	7 ..16 ..3
3 ..18 ..2 reproduisent net	3 ..18 ..2	3 ..18 ..2
1 ..19 ..1 reproduisent net	1 ..19 ..1	1 ..19 ..1
0 ..19 ..6 reproduisent net	0 ..19 ..6	0 ..19 ..6
0 ..9 ..9 reproduisent net	0 ..9 ..9	0 ..9 ..9
0 ..5 ..0 reproduisent net	0 ..5 ..0	0 ..5 ..0
0 ..2 ..6 reproduisent net	0 ..2 ..6	0 ..2 ..6
0 ..1 ..3 reproduisent net	0 ..1 ..3	0 ..1 ..3
0 ..0 ..8 reproduisent net	0 ..0 ..8	0 ..0 ..8
Total 2000.tt ..0 ..0	Total 2000.tt ..0 ..0	Total 2000.tt ..0 ..0

Il n'est pas nécessaire de s'attacher a l'intelligence de ce Tableau avant la lecture des 7 premiers Chapitres, il suffit a chaque chapitre de faire attention a la partie du Tableau qui y a rapport.

Facsimile of a page from the luxury edition of the Tableau économique, as part of "Elemens de la Philosophie rurale," by Marquis de Mirabeau (1767).

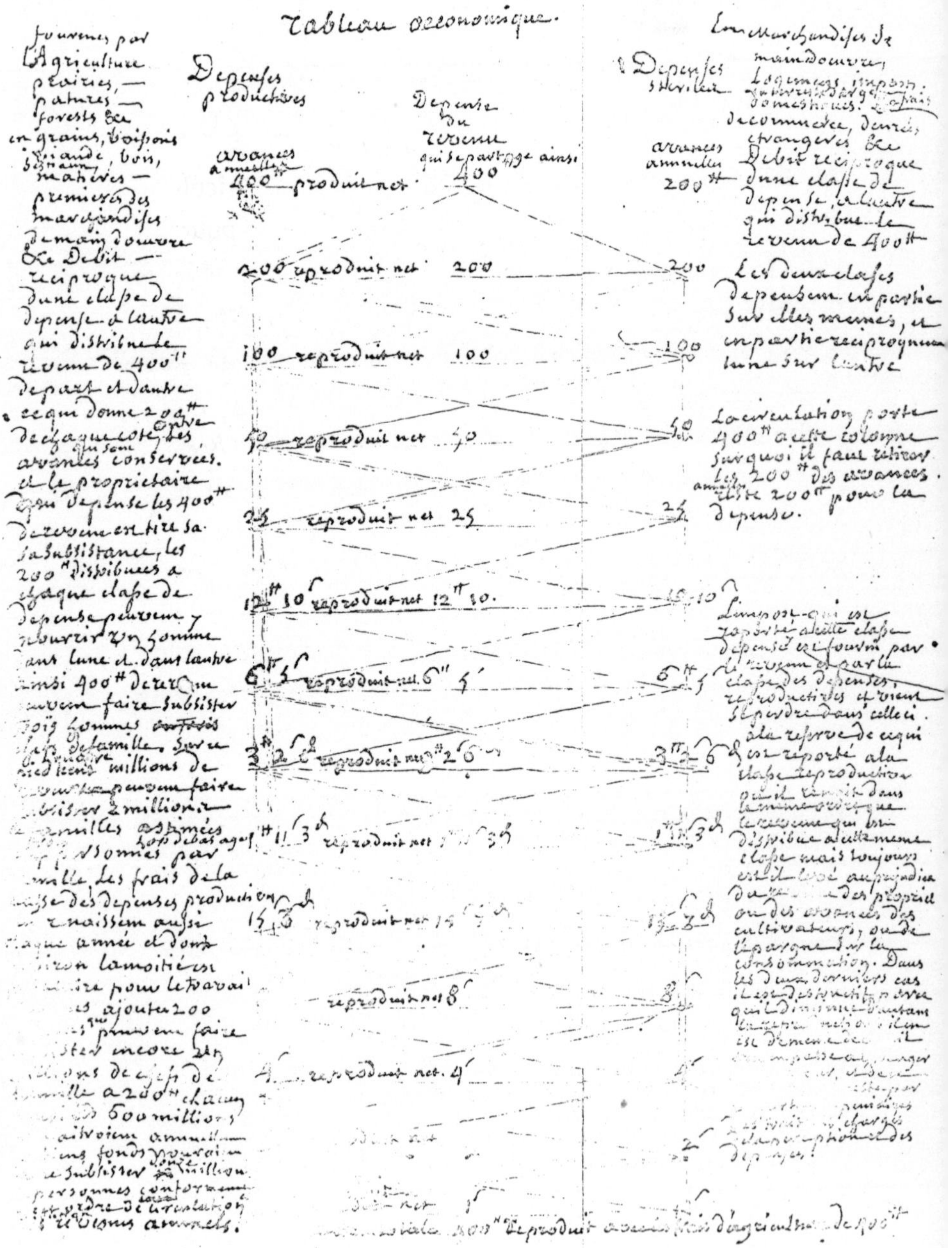

Oldest by the hand of Quesnay made sketch of the Tableau économique, found among the library estate of Marquis V. de Mirabeau, Archives Nationale, Paris, M. 784.

EXPLICATION
DU TABLEAU ÉCONOMIQUE.

LES *Dépenses productives* sont employées à l'agriculture, prairies, pâtures, forêts, mines, pêche, &c. pour perpétuer les richesses, en grains, boissons, bois, bestiaux, matières premières des ouvrages de main-d'œuvre, &c.

Les *Dépenses stériles* se font en marchandises de main-d'œuvre, logemens, vetemens, intérêts d'argent, domestiques, frais de commerce, denrées étrangères, &c.

La vente du produit net que le Cultivateur a fait naître l'année précédente, par le moyen des *Avances annuelles* de 600 liv. employées à la culture par le Fermier, fournit au Propriétaire le payement d'un *revenu* de 600 livres.

Les *avances annuelles* de 300 liv. des dépenses stériles sont employées pour les fonds & les frais du commerce, pour les achats de matière première d'ouvrage de main-d'œuvre, & pour la subsistance & autres besoins de l'artisan, jusqu'à ce qu'il ait achevé & vendu son ouvrage.

Les *600 liv. de revenu* sont dépensées par le Propriétaire, moitié à la classe des dépenses productives en pain, vin, viande, &c. & l'autre moitié à la classe des dépenses stériles en vêtemens, emmeublemens, ustensiles, &c.

Ces dépenses peuvent se porter plus ou moins d'un côté ou de l'autre, selon que celui qui les fait se livre plus ou moins au luxe de subsistance, ou au luxe de décoration. On a pris ici l'état moyen où les dépenses reproductives renouvellent d'année en année le même revenu. Mais on

From an original copy of 1759 with Quesnay's manuscript notes, discovered among the papers of the elder Mirabeau in the Archives Nationale at Paris. The original edition was privately printed at the palace of Versailles by Louis XV and Mme. Pompadour on their hand press. It was issued in exceedingly small numbers and these appear to have been carefully suppressed.

TABLEAU ECONOMIQUE.

Objets à considérer, 1°. Trois sortes de dépenses; 2°. leur source; 3°. leurs avances; 4° leur distribution; 5°. leurs effets; 6°. leur reproduction; 7°. leurs rapports entr'elles; 8°. leurs rapports avec la population; 9° avec l'Agriculture; 10.° avec l'industrie; 11.° avec le commerce; 12°. avec la masse des richesses d'une Nation.

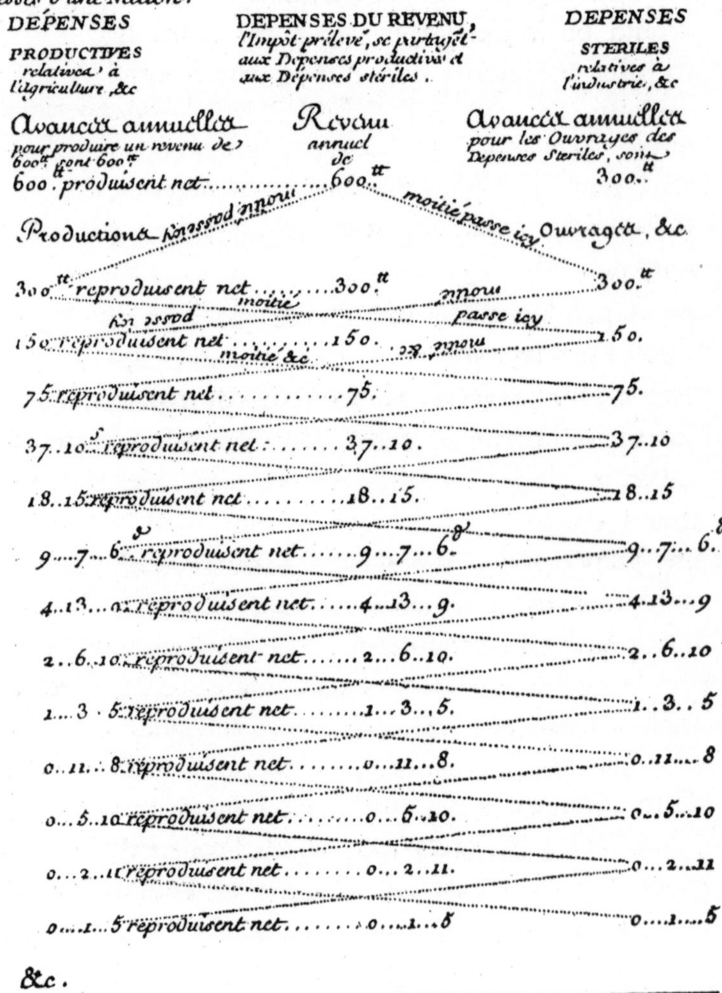

REPRODUIT TOTAL .... 600.tt de revenu; de plus, les frais annuels de 600.tt et les interets des avances primitives du Laboureur, de 300.tt que la terre restitue. Ainsi la réproduction est de 1500.tt compris le revenu de 600.tt qui est la base du calcul, abstraction faite de l'impôt prélevé, et des avances qu'exige sa reproduction annuelle, &c. Voyez l'Explication à la page suivante.

as prepoſterous in the Dutch to encourage agriculture above traffick, and in the Poles traffick above agriculture, and in the people of Geneva either above manufactures, as it would be in our government, for example, to offer premiums for raiſing the greateſt quantity of corn within the bills of mortality, or for inſtructing the greateſt number of country boys in navigation and accompts, or for promoting agriculture and traffick within the liberties of ſuch a place as Mancheſter, too ſmall, and too remote from the channels of communication between other places, to yield employment to any of her hands in either one or the other of theſe branches of buſineſs, and, therefore, fit only for acting that part in the body politic, which ſhe actually does, with ſo much advantage to herſelf, and to every other fellow-member.

But I muſt here take notice, that by the word, *traffick*, I do not mean the buying from ſtrangers to ſell to fellow-ſubjects, or from fellow-ſubjects to ſell to ſtrangers; a branch of buſineſs in all places uſeful, and in many abſolutely eſſential to their existence. What I mean by *traffick*, to adopt my author's meaning of that word, is the buying from strangers to sell to strangers; that business, in short, which is at present chiefly carried on by the Dutch, as it was formerly by the Hanse-towns, the Venetians, and the Genoese; but without which, thank God, Great Britain can subsist better on her tillage and her manufactures, than it was ever possible for these states to do on their extensive traffick. Accordingly, though some writers of eminence have affected to consider her as one of the greatest trafficking nations in the world, she is, if we consider things rightly, very far from being so, at least proportionably to her extent. She consumes herself almost all her own imports, and of course exports little else but her own produce: super-eminently happy in thus having within herself almost all the materials of her happiness, at least such a redundancy of some, as easily to obtain in exchange what she wants of others; such an abundance of the most useful things, as to afford plentiful roots of that internal strength so necessary to keep out an enemy; such a defect of some others, as cannot

be

be ſupplied but by thoſe means, which, to iſlanders eſpecially, are requiſite to keep him at a diſtance, and withal maintain that correſpondence with the reſt of mankind, without which the moſt civilized nations could not but in time relapſe into their primitive barbariſm. She is both miſtreſs and ſervant. Her own hands and lands ſupply her with all the neceſſaries, and almoſt all the conveniencies of life. She is, as a ſtate, in the ſame condition, that the prophet wiſhed to be as an individual. She is neither poor, like ſome petty trading ſtates, obliged to ſlave for others, and often tempted to oppreſs them; nor extravagantly opulent, like Mexico or Peru, which, by having it in their power to procure every thing by the labour of ſlaves, are enervated beyond the poſſibility of reſiſting any power that ſhould ſeriouſly attempt to enſlave themſelves; ſuppoſing them to be actually free, which, by the bye, is very far from being the caſe.

But, to return. Some perſons may think, that ſuch obvious truths did not require to be demonſtrated; but thoſe, who think ſo, muſt,

muſt, ſurely, have read very few of our reputedly beſt authors upon trade and commerce, moſt of whom, conſidering only the flouriſhing condition of ſome confined, tho' well ſituated, trading ſtate, as more within their track, hold it forth as an univerſal example, and propoſe traffick as the only ſource of happineſs in every other, and conſequently the only object worth the legiſlature's attention in all. But theſe examples of theirs, upon which they ſhape all their flimſy arguments, not to ſpeak of the arguments themſelves, are refuted in the following ſheets by other examples. We ſhall there find by the pictures of France at different periods, that, even making allowances for the ravages of war, ſhe could, in the beginning of the reign of Lewis XIV. when ſhe had no traffick, and very little commercial communication, at leaſt in her own bottoms, with other nations, boaſt, in conſequence of the ſuperior attention paid to agriculture, or rather the ſuperior eaſe her farmers were permitted to enjoy in point of taxes and military ſervice, a greater number of inhabitants, and a greater proportion of them happy, than when that

that monarch, at the inſtigation of Monſieur Colbert, endeavoured to make France another Holland, or rather the only ſeat of commerce and manufactures to the excluſion of all the other nations of Europe; as though it were not, in a manner, impoſſible to render any very extenſive country, like France, as populous as Holland, by any other means than agriculture, which, in this wild project, was, however, totally overlooked, or rather ſacrificed to ſupport it. And unleſs ſuch a country was equally populous, how is it poſſible, that ſhe ſhould be proportionably ſtrong in trade and manufactures?

It is this error, chiefly, with regard to France, that the author of the following œconomical table, and the FRIEND OF MANKIND, who has taken upon him to explain that table, endeavour to refute. How they have acquitted themſelves of this taſk, we may gueſs by the encomiums beſtowed on their work by the foreign Journaliſts and Reviewers, and judge for ourſelves by examining it. But, though the reaſonings employed for this purpoſe have, as I have

have already intimated, an eye chiefly, if not altogether, to France, they may be eaſily applied, affirmatively to every country of an extenſive and fruitful ſoil, and negatively to every other, ſo as to conſtitute an univerſal rule of conduct for all.

THIS rule, however, the Marquis, I muſt own, has left open to ſome objections, eſpecially from thoſe who love the fine arts, as every man muſt to be allowed any pretenſions to thought and feeling. He inſiſts, that agriculture cannot poſſibly flouriſh in a country like France, unleſs the bulk of the inhabitants prefer the luxuries of ſubſiſtence to thoſe of decoration, commonly deemed the only ſupport of theſe arts. As, therefore, ſome readers may not be more tender in judging of his meaning, than he has been guarded in expreſſing it, I muſt beg leave to remark, that he is by no means for having the rich ſpend all their money in the purchaſe of the luxuries of ſubſiſtence, as at firſt ſight one might be apt to conclude, inſtead of beſtowing part of it on the poor for the luxuries of decoration; ſince, the poor having mouths as well

well as the rich, the demand in both cafes muft be the fame on the farmer. He does not require that the confumption of the firft products fhould be confined to any particular fet of men; all he requires is, that they fhould be confumed. But confumed, he apprehends, they never would, were a fuperior tafte for the luxuries of decoration univerfally to prevail, even in towns and cities, fince by fuch numbers of people, in that cafe, confining themfelves to the purchafe of manufactures, it would be impoffible for the farmer to fell the produce of his labours, and of courfe to pay his rent, the confequence of which muft naturally be an almoft total ceffation of agriculture, the deftruction of the landed intereft; and, to go a ftep farther than my authors perhaps intended, an end of every fublunary enjoyment worthy the wifh of a rational being.

For, not to fpeak of that fuper-eminently ufeful and entertaining employment which agriculture affords the mind of man, and which it ever affords in proportion as it is cultivated, what fine art is there, that

can

can yield the ſenſes half the ſatisfaction which they derive from agriculture? Can any ornaments, within the narrow bounds of our tenements, compare with thoſe diffuſible by agriculture over the immenſe face of nature? Nay, it is a queſtion, if theſe ornaments could ſo much as ſubſiſt without it; for where, without agriculture, could the fine arts find either objects or patterns to work upon, ſince, if all were wildneſs, wildneſs would have no charms? Beſides, it is not to be expected, that a taſte, however ſtrong, for the luxuries of decoration alone, ſhould ever occaſion thoſe tempeſts in the human breaſt, thoſe buſtles in ſociety, thoſe ſtruggles between nature and art, which afford the nobleſt ſubjects to the pencil, the chiſſel, and even the pen itſelf, to rank poetry and oratory among the fine arts? It may, therefore, be affirmed, that even good eating and drinking is but the laſt ſcene of a long ſeries of pleaſures of a much higher order neceſſary to furniſh it; but for which, were it not for the ſake of the laſt, the generality of mankind would not, it may be preſumed, think it worth their while to take any pains.

pains. In what age, or country, for inſtance, have thoſe moſt pleaſing arts of planting and plowing, of grazing cattle and feeding poultry, with all the other amuſing details of a country-life, been practiſed to any degree, merely to enliven the creation, perfume the air, and give freſh and blooming looks, and an ever-youthful countenance, to the earth? No! in this reſpect, mankind is always a child. For, as it is often neceſſary to inflict ſome ſmall evils on children to make them avoid great ones; ſo is it neceſſary to hold out ſome coarſe enjoyments to mankind, to make it attend to thoſe of a refined nature.

But, allowing uncultivated nature alone ſufficient to ſupply the arts of decoration with ſubjects and patterns, what would it ſignify, were the human fancy unable to operate properly upon them. And that this would be the caſe, without mankind's enjoying the luxuries, and conſequently cultivating the arts, of ſubſiſtence, is plain both from our own feelings and the example and authority even of thoſe, who have ſucceeded beſt in cultivating the arts of decoration.

decoration. Not to ſpeak of all that philanthropy of ſentiment, that hilarity of thought, that gaiety of countenance, that freedom of converſation, almoſt inſeparable from a plentiful table, and thoſe ſo happily expreſſed *libera vina* of Horace, as conſtituting in themſelves, in the opinion of the ſame poet, one of the moſt pleaſing ſubjects of verſe, what other ſubjects of verſe could be properly celebrated without it? According to Juvenal, Horace himſelf required to be brim-full to call upon the Muſes to any purpoſe; and all Virgil's fire would have produced nothing but ſmoke, had he not enjoyed his ſhare of the conveniencies of life. Nay, the Royal Pſalmiſt himſelf, though he declares, that, to ſee the glory of the Moſt Higheſt, he found it requiſite to appear before him as in a dry, barren, wild, and deſart land; yet a little lower in the ſame Pſalm he ſays, that, in praiſing and exalting even that glory, he found ſomething operate on his ſoul like *marrow and fatneſs*; emphatically alluding to that material ſatiety ſo requiſite duly to deſcribe and celebrate all material ſubjects.

LET

LET us go a ſtep farther, and grant, that, without cultivating the arts of ſubſiſtence, the arts of decoration, and, if we may continue to conſider them as arts, thoſe tranſcendent ones of oratory and poetry, could ſubſiſt, to what purpoſe would it be, if mankind itſelf, for want of cultivating the arts of ſubſiſtence, ſhould decline by degrees, and at laſt ſet never to riſe again? To what purpoſe would colours be, if there were no eyes; or muſic, if there were no ears; or odours, if there were no organs of ſmell? Now, nothing can be plainer, than it is from obſervation, that farmers are the only claſs of people, who not only keep up their own numbers, but make amends for the ravages that happen in all the other claſſes of mankind, particularly thoſe employed in the arts of decoration. Hence it is, that ſo few families in the inland and ſecond-rate towns, even of England, can trace their pedigrees three or four generations back, without finding themſelves in the fields. Hence it is, that, the arts of decoration being ſo much cultivated in England, the cultivation of thoſe of ſubſiſtence, though very great, is ſcarcely able to keep up our numbers; whereas in our North-American colonies, where few arts are known but thoſe of ſubſiſtence, the inhabitants, double, even independent of any acceſſions from abroad, every five and twenty or thirty years. Nor is it the number of mankind alone, that would thus dwindle without the cultivation of the arts of ſubſiſtence; its powers and its beauties both mental and corporeal would infallibly ſuffer a proportionable decay. Farming is the only kind of life, in which every thing concurs, not only to encreaſe, but to improve the ſpecies, or at leaſt keep it up to its original ſtandard; open air; exerciſe of body and mind without exhauſtion; plenty without exceſs; a conſtant proſpect of the unceaſing operations of nature, the Almighty's handmaid, ſo well adapted to illuſtrate, and keep up the remembrance of, His own immediate operations in the grand works of creation and renovation, and thereby fill the mind with ſentiments of reſpect, love, and gratitude towards that all-perfect Being, and conſequently of benevolence to all thoſe, whom, from equal motives of goodneſs, he has choſen to be equally

equally ſharers of the ſame bleſſings; advantages, which, however great in themſelves, muſt, in England, be greatly improved by the farmers conſciouſneſs of their enjoying a free intercourſe with all the other claſſes of the community; and it is, no doubt, to this free intercourſe between the farming and the other claſſes of her inhabitants, that this happy country is indebted for thoſe ſuperior excellencies of body and of mind, by which her children of all ranks are ſo eaſily diſtinguiſhable from the children of every other, even thoſe bleſſed, if any ſuch there are, with the ſame happy combination of ſun and ſoil, liberty and law, on the face of this terreſtrial globe.

However neceſſary, therefore, agriculture may be to France, it is vaſtly more uſeful to England, ſince, though England, on account of the ſuperior number of her ports in proportion to her extent, can do better without agriculture than France, ſhe, on account of her happy conſtitution, receives many more advantages from it. Agriculture, if, in ſome degree, more meat and

and drink to France than to England, is to England, in an almoſt infinite degree, more than to France, health and ſtrength, beauty and comelineſs, thought and ſpirit, induſtry and œconomy, bravery and benevolence, every ingredient, in ſhort, fitteſt to form the manufacturer and the artiſt, the mechanic and the merchant, the man of buſineſs and the man of letters, the philoſopher and the legiſlator, the friend as well as the maſter of mankind. Wherefore, O Engliſhmen, (I was going to ſay, at your peril, but I cannot help ſaying) as ye tender your own happineſs, that of your poſterity, and even that of mankind, look with an eye of ſuperlative complacency upon farming, and countenance and encourage by every poſſible allowance of eaſe, profit, and honor, all thoſe concerned in ſo greatly and ſo univerſally beneficial a profeſſion.

THE

THE CONTENTS OF THE OECONOMICAL TABLE.

INTRODUCTION page 1

PART I.

Sect. I.

The Oeconomical Table *considered in its Construction* page 21

Sect. II.

The Oeconomical Table *considered in its Progress* p. 29

Sect. III.

The Oeconomical Table *considered relatively to Populousness* page 39

Sect. IV.

The Oeconomical Table *considered relatively to the Amount of the Impost and Tithes* p. 49

Sect.

Sect. V.

The Oeconomical Table *considered relatively to the National Cash* p. 61

Sect. VI.

The Oeconomical Table *considered in the Estimation of the Produce and capital Stock of every Kind of Riches* p. 71

Sect. VII.

The Oeconomical Table *considered in the Conditions necessary to the free Play and Prosperity of the political Machine* p. 83

PART II.

Sect. I.

The Oeconomical Table *considered in its private Depredations. Excess of* Luxury p. 97

Sect. II.

The Oeconomical Table *considered relatively to Spoliation* p. 113

Sect. III.

The Oeconomical Table, *in which the Decay of Husbandry, and the ſad Effects of ſuch Declenſion, relatively to Population, are diſplayed* p. 125

Sect. IV.

The Oeconomical Table *conſidered in its Diſorders relatively to Money* p. 137

Sect. V.

The Oeconomical Table *conſidered in its Diſorders relatively to the Police* p. 151

Sect. VI.

The Oeconomical Table *conſidered in its Depredations relatively to Commerce* p. 163

Sect. VII.

The Oeconomical Table *conſidered in its Depredations relatively to the Impoſt* p. 175

The CONCLUSION p. 198

The RECAPITULATION p. 201

This

This excellent work is the *Ne plus ultra* of the œconomical ſcience, the moſt important of all the ſciences. It, therefore, ſhould be read and diligently ſtudied by all thoſe, who are deſirous of acquiring juſt ideas concerning the real and imaginary riches of a ſtate; of thoroughly underſtanding the nature of circulation; of diſtinguiſhing expence from luxury; of knowing what rank nominal values deſerve in political ſpeculations; and of deciding with juſtneſs concerning the propriety of the ſeveral laws, cuſtoms, and regulations of a country. It is, in a manner, impoſſible to give any abſtract of a work, that is, itſelf, an abſtract of principles and demonſtrations, which, handled as fully as they ought to be, would alone ſuffice to fill volumes.

Journal des Sçavans for *February* 1761.

THE

THE

OECONOMICAL TABLE.

INTRODUCTION.

HUMAN ſcience, properly ſpeaking, conſiſts in the knowledge of human affairs. Theſe lie all under our eyes, or within our reach, and the ſimpleſt notions concerning them are the neareſt to truth; but our underſtanding is weak, and too apt, when obliged to compare and combine its ideas, to give way under the burthen, and warp from its erect poſture.

ART ſhould never interfere in our ſearch after truth, but as an index to point her out, or as a light to direct our notions in the pur ſuit of her, whenever the croud of relations between intereſts, remote from each other, happens to dazzle and diſtract our underſtanding. But now become an inſtrument of illuſion, it fills us with borrowed and erroneous opinions: it builds in the air, like the architects of NECTANEBO, and not only robs us of our direct feelings, and of our natural ideas, but likewiſe, by a neceſſary conſequence, of the great advantages we might expect from a more regular conduct, and from that aſſiſtance, which nature never refuſes to thoſe, who allow things to follow her direction.

IT is chiefly in the œconomical ſcience, that never-failing ſource of our ſubſiſtence, of our manners, and, in ſhort, of every thing that can with any propriety be called the object of that fundamental ſcience, the ſcience of governing well, that this fatal inconvenience is moſt ſeverely felt. Man, who learns nothing but like a child, who never ſees in religion any preſent and immediate retribution of virtue and vice; who never attributes obedience

obedience to any thing but habit or intereſt; never conſiders manners but as the fruits of a good education; who, in a word, never looks deeper than the ſurface in moral matters; man, I ſay, guilty of all theſe miſtakes in affairs of ſuch importance, commits the ſame in thoſe, which are purely phyſical. The art of over-reaching he dignifies with the name of policy; a heap of counters with that of riches; civil piracy, with that of finance; the knack of bartering to advantage, with that of commerce. And behold! he has no ſooner crammed theſe notions into his brain, in confuſed and ill-ſorted bundles, but he ſets out to perplex himſelf and his cotemporaries; and ſelf-love and intereſt find it ſo much the eaſier to uſurp the reins of his underſtanding in matters relating to his peculiar ſphere of life, as the crude notions, upon which theſe partial ſyſtems are built, have no manner of foundation in judgment or truth.

For inſtance. Of all the writers upon commerce, who ſwarmed in ſuch numbers when that ſubject happened to be in vogue, how many began by untying the bundle marked with that grand word, COMMERCE; by diſtinguiſhing properly between the trade carried on in the firſt neceſſaries of life, the trade carried on in the immediate fruits of the earth, and the trade carried on in manufactures; between that trade, which conſiſts in carrying for foreigners, and that, which conſiſts in buying in one foreign country to ſell in another; between the trade carried on by means of metals, and that carried on by means of paper; between the trade carried on by individuals, and the trade carried on by companies, *&c.* Has any of them taken the leaſt trouble to diſtinguiſh between the profits, which thoſe, who carry on a foreign trade, make upon their fellow-ſubjects, and thoſe they make upon foreigners, and then aſcertain the amount of theſe ſeveral profits? Has any of them been at the pains of calculating, how far the nation is benefitted by the firſt; and of forming a judgment of the viſible or hidden ſtate of theſe different gains, though abſolutely neceſſary to make a juſt repartition of taxes? No! we are as yet unacquainted

quainted with all theſe details. We are perpetually confounding the produce of the earth with the produce of trade; nay, we think the former beneath our notice, and, inſtead of relying on the huſbandman, expect every thing at the hands of the merchant and manufacturer, though by no means ſo nearly related to us. Every thing goes under the name of trade, the ſupport of ſtates, the ſource of ſplendor, and the like rhetorical amplifications. Not one author has as yet conſidered the origin and tendency of all theſe things. Hence miſtakes in the principles, and ruin in the conſequences, of our conduct.

THE ſame may be ſaid of all the other parts of our preſent theory of human affairs, which, as well as trade, are but ſo many branches of that great phyſical ſcience of this earthly globe, the œconomical ſcience.

Is it not ſurpriſing, or rather ſhocking, to think, that this ſcience of ſciences is as yet without profeſſors, or adepts, or genuine principles! I do not wonder that primitive men, this moment obedient to the laws of nature, the next ſlaves to the firſt ſallies of human pride, ſhould have taken it into their heads, that the primary notions of ſubſiſtence could not fail of being perpetuated in all their purity, by the mere empire of neceſſity; that the Egyptians, who all at once became ſo powerful and ſo wiſe a nation, in conſequence of their ſeeking for proſperity in the arts from which it originally ſprings, namely, thoſe of agriculture, have left us no traces of their reſearches this way, involved in hieroglyphics, agreeable to the genius of the eaſtern people; that the Greeks, born to cultivate thoſe arts which are the daughters of the imagination, and ſcattered over a barren ſoil, ſhould have deſpiſed the fundamental ſcience in the government of nations, and ſhould have cheriſhed no more of it than ſuited their love of liberty and of pleaſure; that the Romans, firſt warriors, next conquerors, then plunderers, and at laſt a prey to plunderers, ſhould have regarded nothing in the æconomical ſcience but its independency, and ſhould have left us nothing concerning it, but a few inſtructions

in

in practical agriculture, without ever considering this source of riches, in its essential relations to the constituent form of states: I easily conceive how all this has happened. But that, since arts and sciences have civilized the western world, since Europe, divided into nations well known to each other, governed by equitable laws, made sisters by trade, and rescued from tyranny and slavery by a religion powerful to conquer and subdue the most attrocious passions; since every corner of Europe, I say, can boast of men greedy of praise, and expecting it only in proportion to their endeavours to serve mankind; since the sciences compose a kind of universe, and the *republic of letters* is an expression in every mouth; that within this period, I say, the learned and the wise, convinced that a man may make himself useful by his studies, should notwithstanding have applied themselves to every thing, except what ought to be the first and chief concern of us mortals; this it is that I am utterly at a loss to account for. Let such, as imagine that illiterate and rote-taught rustics, are equal to this science, but cast an eye on our table, and they will ſoon ſee their miſtake. As to the notion of this ſcience belonging to none but men ſeated at the helm of affairs, I dare affirm, that thoſe, who govern, have no time to do any thing elſe. They muſt have a chain of principles ready formed to their hands. The maxims and details, ſo neceſſary to form the ſtateſman, depend on the general connection and order of natural effects, which carry along with them the whole political maſs, by the indiſſoluble concatenation of all the moral and phyſical concerns of this our ſublunary world. It is the inveſtigation of theſe principles, that the philoſophers, engaged in the ſtudy of nature, ſhould make the object of their meditations. It is the reſult of ſuch inveſtigation, demonſtrated in the cleareſt manner, that compoſes the ſcience of government. This ſtudy conſiſts in a practical and deciſive knowledge of ſeveral things, which ought to be examined, ſounded, and developed by the learned, whom ſuch uſeful labours would entitle to the eſteem and thanks of mankind. May not the man, who has ſacrificed immenſe calculations

calculations to the ambition of refolving the Catenarian problem, while we are left in the dark concerning the means of procuring our daily bread, concerning the concurrence of all thofe œconomical functions fitteft to fecure fubfiftence and power to a nation; may not, I fay, fuch an idle genius be compared to the father of a family, who aimed at nothing, ftudied nothing, ambitioned nothing, but to become an able chefs-player. O ye, whom Providence has diftinguifhed by her richeft gifts, confider, I befeech you, that it could by no means be her intention in fo doing, to confine you to the poor fatisfaction of making a figure in the eyes of a lazy and curious people. All the hours you throw away on fuch idle fpeculations, is fo much time ftolen from the ftudy of a patriot, and the duty of a citizen. The fcience now before us is the province of the learned, for a man muft be learned indeed, to dive to the bottom of it. Yes, the œconomical fcience is of fuch extent, her objects are fo numerous, her relations fo intricate, that her interpreters, to fucceed in the development and combination of fo many

branches

branches of knowledge, cannot be too well practiſed in the ſtudy of the abſtruſe ſciences; and yet you leave me, me whoſe negligence of ſtyle, and exuberance of ideas, you ſo juſtly condemn; you leave me, I ſay, to wander alone in this new and ſtrange road. For ſhame, awake! awake, I ſay, from that profound lethargy, in which you thus ignobly ſuffer yourſelf to be held by the charms of ſome more agreeable occupation. Awake! ariſe! ſhew yourſelves in the employment moſt worthy of your ſuperior talents; or, when you ſee princes degenerate into tyrants, power abuſed to ſerve the worſt of purpoſes, men blind to every thing but their own intereſt, the poor oppreſſed and ſtarving on the dunghill, ſubſiſtence refuſed to beings like yourſelves, and the race of Japhet juſtly branded with the appellation of *a cruel and mercileſs brood*; ceaſe to attribute to guilt, that which proceeds merely from ignorance; ceaſe to accuſe human nature, it is yourſelves alone you are to accuſe. Yes, preſent your heads to the vengeful thunderbolt, and ſay, what the mother of a tyrant formerly ſaid; *It is here you ſhould ſtrike.*

ſtrike. Say; "Had we pointed out to "mankind the road of phyſical profit and "moral good, united and combined toge- "ther, they would have purſued them; at "leaſt we ſhould not be anſwerable for "their miſtakes."

BUT things are not quite ſo bad; this ſcience begins to gain notice. I have met not only fellow-labourers, as hinted elſe- where, but even guides in the purſuit of it: a man of genius, who has analized and minutely examined all the principles of it, and by this ſtudy has diſcovered the ſource of all thoſe evils, with which nations often find themſelves overwhelmed, when they think themſelves wiſeſt, has laboured, by a cloſe and obſtinate application ſuitable to his talents, to acquire juſt and ſolid ideas of the ſource, progreſs, and employment of riches. But on marſhalling in his head the reſult of theſe ideas, he ſaw plainly that it was impoſſible to communicate them pro- perly by the mere invention of letters, with- out making out a map or drawing to aſſiſt them; and it is to this conviction of his we owe the following œconomical table. But though I perfectly agree with him in the principles upon which he has constructed it, I could not, with all the application I was maſter of, comprehend theſe principles in their full extent, till I had made out a map myſelf, and withal drawn up ſome explanations of that map for my own uſe. It is theſe explanations, ſuited to my own, and conſequently to the weakeſt capacity, which I now offer to the public, for whoſe uſe I received the ingenious performance that is the object of them.

I MUST however, before I go any further, beg leave to obſerve, that ſuch, as do not chuſe to beſtow a little cloſe and patient thinking on this performance, had as good never look into it, ſince otherwiſe, in all probability, they would ſoon loſe the thread of the writers arguments, and reap nothing but error for their trouble. As for my part, I could not explain myſelf more fully, without diluting too much this maſs of principles, which, though capable of furniſhing matter for a thouſand volumes,

cannot

cannot at firſt be kept too cloſe together. I muſt, above all things, caution the reader againſt flattering himſelf that he underſtands the table, till he has read the explanations of it, in all the different lights and points of view, in which he will here find it diſplayed.

BUT before we ſet out, we would do well to lay down to ourſelves a few fundamental axioms, viz.

THE earth is the mother of all our goods.

OF theſe goods, whatever is conſumed by him, who cultivates the earth, is ſubſiſtence, and nothing riches, but what he can diſpoſe of.

THE man, who cultivates the earth with his hands, can expect no more from it than barely ſubſiſtence for himſelf and his family, and that too of the pooreſt kind. He muſt therefore look out for ſuch aſſiſtants, as may procure him a greater produce, and at the ſame time require leſs to maintain them.

THIS

This aſſiſtance conſiſts in machines, in cattle, in manures, &c. Theſe things are not to be had without money, and the amount of what they coſt is what we ſhall call the huſbandman's primitive advances.

As of theſe things, ſome, viz. the cattle, muſt have graſs, corn, &c. and all in general are ſubject to wear and tear, proper allowances muſt be made to ſupport, repair, and recruit them. Now this allowance, added to the huſbandman's ſubſiſtence, conſtitutes what we ſhall call the huſbandman's annual advances, ſince he muſt every year feed and recruit his live ſtock, and till and ſow his land, &c. before he can expect any crop from it.

A good crop, ſuch as may be expected from a good cultivation, ſhould yield, 1ſt, A reimburſement of the annual advances, in order to enable the huſbandman to prepare in time for, and lay the foundations, as it were, of the next year's crop. 2dly, The intereſt of his primitive and annual advances, that is, a decent profit on the funds employed by by him in machines, cattle, manures, &c. 3dly, A further return which the husbandman may sell or barter.

It is this last portion of the annual produce, which we call income: it is the only portion that can be called riches, the rest being indispensably requisite to keep agoing the œconomical machine.

It is upon this portion, thus proved to be *riches*, and which we shall call *income*, that all the œconomical contexture of society depends. It is this portion that yields, 1st, Tithes, consecrated to the support of the altar; 2dly, The public revenue, set apart for the government and defence of the community; 3dly, The landlord's rent, being what the husbandman pays him for his land, free from all the charges of cultivating it.

Of these three portions, the first affords directly a livelihood to all those engaged in the service of religion; the second, a livelihood to all those inlisted in the service of the public; the third, a livelihood to the landlord,

landlord, and all thoſe employed in his ſervice.

THE three together, and each of them ſeparately, maintain indirectly, and by the tribute of neceſſity, all the working part of the nation, as well huſbandmen as manufacturers; ſo that this working part of the nation, which before harveſt had nothing to live upon but their advances, live afterwards upon the *income*, which flows back to them to purchaſe their ſuperfluities, and affords them the means of pouring it back in their turn upon others that have any thing to ſpare, which they, the working part of the nation, want, and have not reaped from the earth, or manufactured.

SUCH is the machine of circulation in all its parts, here repreſented by money; which, in itſelf, is no ſubſiſtence, but merely an inſtrument of barter univerſally adopted by all nations.

THIS is the circulation repreſented by the table, which I am now going to lay before the

the reader, and the explanations of which he will do well to attend to in the order I ſhall give them.

THIS table ſhews, that, by means of the circulation between the three claſſes, viz. the proprietary claſs, conſiſting of the church, the ſtate, and the landlord; the productive claſs, conſiſting of thoſe employed in tilling the earth; and the manufacturing claſs; the circulating maſs appears double the real maſs laid out in advances.

BUT we muſt carefully diſtinguiſh the phyſical point of riches, which is reproduction, without which there would be no holding out above one year.

THUS, then, it appears, that riches have but one root, and that this root is the productive claſs, which vivifies all the other claſſes, giving them forces that return back to itſelf, doubled by the favourable impulſe of a briſk, equable, and in every other reſpect well regulated circulation.

Now, it is this circulation we are to conſider in the table, whoſe fourteen ſub-diviſions, though they appear gradual, are, in fact, merely diſtributive; for it is in one and the ſame year, that all this repartition amongſt all the numberleſs ramifications of ſociety is performed.

But it was by no means the Author's intention to make an algebraical affair of this repartition, and conſider it in all the aſpects of which it is capable. This would be rather a geometrical amuſement, foreign to his object. He has exhibited it in a table, under no other aſpects than ſuch as he thought indiſpenſably requiſite. By doing more he might have rendered it too intricate.

By underſtanding the table, the Reader will readily come to underſtand the depredations into which it is ſuppoſed the circulation may fall; he may be ſure, beſides, of ſeeing his trouble, to make himſelf thorough maſter of the principles flowing from this œconomical ſtudy, amply rewarded not only by the certainty

certainty of the conclusions afforded by them; but by a facility of foresight concerning the nature and effects of every kind of political operations.

In regard to the calculations, it is well known, that such things have always an *errors excepted* tacked to them. The truths, contained in the table, depend not on the *quantum* of those hieroglyphs called cyphers. They have been made use of in the table, which, at first sight, will appear the most intricate part of the work, merely to facilitate the comprehension of it. The eyes must be spoke to in support of the language suited to the mind, which is subject to distraction, but may be called back by mechanical objects. In short, the demonstrator, when not understood any where else, will own the fault to be entirely his; but, if not understood here, must attribute it entirely to the want of attention in the Reader.

THE OECONOMICAL TABLE.

PART I.

SECTION I.

The OECONOMICAL TABLE *confidered in its Conftruction.*

[See TABLE N° I.]

IT was firft neceffary to afcertain whence the income arifes, in what manner it is diftributed among the different claffes of fociety, in what places it vanifhes, and in what it is reproduced.

FOR

FOR this purpoſe the Author makes uſe of three columns. The right hand column comprehends the productive expences, that is to ſay, thoſe of the huſbandman; the left hand column, the barren expences, that is to ſay, thoſe of the manufacturer; the middle column is that of the income, whoſe reflux upon the right and left hand columns ſets and keeps the whole machine of circulation a-going, and affords all the juices requiſite for the ſubſiſtence and encreaſe of the body politic.

THE Author here aſſumes, by way of example, an annual rent of 30 *l.* which he conſiders independently of the land-tax and tithes to avoid perplexity from too many figures; but we may, if we pleaſe, look upon theſe thirty pounds as ſo many millions.

HE has likewiſe aſſumed a kingdom in a flouriſhing ſtate of cultivation, where the reproductive expences yield the ſame income from year to year, that is to ſay, where agriculture affords to the landlord, the king, and the church, in all kinds of produce, combined

combined one with another, one hundred per cent. profit on the annual advances bestowed upon it, besides an interest of ten per cent. on these and the primitive advances; or where the acre of land yields, on an average, 10 *s.* a year rent to the landlord, 5 *s.* for the land-tax, and 2 *s.* 6 *d.* for tithes, in all 17 *s.* 6 *d.* and likewise an equal sum for the reimbursement of the annual advances, besides 10 *s.* 1 *d.* for the interest of the primitive and annual advances; so that the whole annual yield of the acre must be at least 2 *l.* 5 *s.* 1 *d.* taking one year with another, and one kind of crop with another kind. For the acre should produce double that sum the year it is sown with wheat, in order to make amends for the preceeding year that it lay fallow, so that a crop of wheat takes in two years. Thus therefore in the hypothesis of a neat produce of cent. per cent. with the ten per cent. interest on the primitive and annual expences, this crop of wheat should amount to 4 *l.* 10 *s.* 2 *d.* and the crop of spring corn to 2 *l.* 5 *s.* 1 *d.* the acre. But wheat both requires a great deal more charges in proportion, and produces in proportion a great deal more than ſpring corn; ſo that the produce of an acre under wheat ought to be valued at 5 *l.* 10 *s.* 2 *d.* and that of an acre under ſpring corn at 1 *l.* 5 *s.* 1 *d.* amounting to the ſame thing on the whole, that is, 6 *l.* 15 *s.* 3 *d.* the acre, for three years.

OUR ſyſtem excludes the petty kind of culture with oxen, &c. This kind of culture, to which huſbandmen are reduced for want of funds for the primitive advances required by a ſtout culture, is carried on entirely at the expence of the land itſelf. The hay yielded by the meadows of a farm is eat up by the oxen; a great part of the lands is employed in paſturage and other uſes, ſuffered to be fallow, or quite idle, &c. under pretence of giving it time to recover itſelf; in a word, ſwallowed up by the expences of cultivating it. This kind of culture, I ſay, for want of ſufficient primitive advances, requires exceſſive annual advances to ſubſiſt the great number of hands neceſſary to carry it on, who run away with almoſt the whole produce. This ungrateful culture, which betrays the poverty and portends

tends the ruin of thofe nations where it prevails, has no relation to the order of our table, which we fuppofe conformable to that ftate of things, in which the annual advances, employed on a fuitable fund of primitive advances, yield cent. per cent. profit, befides ten per cent. intereft on themfelves, and the primitive advances.

WE moreover fuppofe the venal value of corn what it ought to be kept up to by a freedom and facility of domeftic and foreign commerce, that is to fay, that wheat is worth 38*s.* the quarter. This condition muft be every where underftood; for without fetting a value on the real price of the immediate fruits of the earth, it is impoffible to form any idea of the ftate of expence, or produce, or income of any nation. Let us now explain more at large, what we here mean by thefe two expreffions, *primitive advances*, and *annual advances*.

BY *primitive advances*, omitted in the table for fear of making it too intricate, we mean what the hufbandman muft lay out, on his entering upon buſineſs, in the purchaſe of cattle, inſtruments, and in other extraordinary charges, which, in a ſtate of high cultivation, ſuch as the table ſuppoſes, cannot, with one year's rent, amount to leſs than 500*l.* on a farm of 120 acres, and one plough to work ſuch a farm with, during the two firſt years; for ſo long muſt the farmer be ſatisfied to labour before he can expect a crop: and all this, excluſive of the ordinary annual advances of 105*l.*

PEOPLE are too ignorant in many places, and it is poverty that makes them ſo, of the prodigious advantage there is in not being too frugal in theſe primitive advances. The earth is a moſt grateful parent. She repays with uſury whatever we lend her, and that in an infinite progreſſion in our favour.

IT is this fund of primitive advances, the neceſſity and importance of which cannot but be ſufficiently felt on the bare mention of them, that we muſt chiefly conſider in an agricole ſtate. Fools and knaves, I know, will cry out, *Men have done nothing but complain*

complain of the badneſs of the times theſe twenty years paſt, and yet rents, tithes, and taxes, come in as uſual. I allow, that the huſbandman, though obliged inſtead of large horſes to make uſe of thoſe of a middling ſize, and from thence to deſcend to hobbies, mules, aſſes, &c. may for ſome time longer make a ſhift to pay one way or another; but it will be by breaking in upon his ſtock, by which means his ruin, from being certain, as it was at firſt, becomes abſolutely irretrievable.

THE *annual advances* are the funds employed every year, and take in two objects, viz. the annual productive expences on the one hand, and the annual barren expences on the other.

THE annual *productive expences* are employed in tillage, meadows, paſture land, fiſheries, mines, and in the ſubſiſtence of the hands belonging to this claſs, &c. in order to perpetuate our riches in corn, beverage, timber, cattle, and materials for the manufacturing claſs, &c.

THE

THE annual *barren expences* take in all the expences of the manufacturing claſs, as well domeſtic, as thoſe requiſite to carry on, or ſubſervient to, their reſpective employments.

THE Author, by making the rent 30*l.* and ſuppoſing it the produce, on the footing of a ſtout culture, of cent. per cent. beſides the intereſts already ſo often mentioned, allows, it is plain, 30*l.* for the annual productive expences: in the ſame hypotheſis, by allowing an expence proportioned to the income in the manufacturing claſs, he fixes the annual advances for the annual barren expences at 15*l.* Let us now examine the diſtribution and circulation of the income, according to the rules juſt laid down.

SECTION

SECTION II.

The OECONOMICAL TABLE *considered in its Progress.*

[See TABLE N° I.]

THE annual advances of 30*l.* committed to the earth by the husbandman, yield him a net produce of 30*l.* for the landlord.

THIS will appear a very idle supposition to the many poor landlords, who think themselves but too happy in meeting with some wretched farmer willing to divide the fruits of every kind with them, and, miserable as these conditions are, they are too good for so paltry a cultivation, since on the least calamity the landlord must support his tenant, or expect to see his lands deserted by him. But this dismal kind of culture, the daughter of necessity, and the

the mother of mifery, has nothing common with a good culture, fuch as may be feen in fome countries, and fuch as we here fuppofe it; where the hufbandman, independent as to his food, receives nothing from the landlord but the canvafs of the produce, and has even his own private fund of primitive annual advances, for which the earth pays him at leaft ten per cent. intereft. This portion of the hufbandman's annual reimburfements, as I have already faid, is not taken notice of in the table; but the Author, in the recapitulation at the bottom of the faid table, allows 17*l.* 5*s.* 8*d.* $\frac{1}{2}$ for the intereft of the primitive and annual advances requifite to yield a rent of 30*l.*

BUT to proceed. The annual advances of 15*l.* fet down here for the barren expences, confift in the purchafe of raw materials for the manufacturer to work upon, and in his fubfiftence, till he has finifhed and fold his goods. But thefe advances reproduce nothing, as every one knows, and the table evinces. Trade and manufactures, I fay, produce nothing, but only give every

thing

thing the greateſt relative value. The 15*l.* net produce, which conſtitute the landlord's rent, are expended by him, half among the claſs of productive expences, for bread, wine, meat, &c. and the other half among the claſs of barren expences, for cloaths, furniture, and the like.

THE 15*l.* of the rent, which, in the order of the table, immediately paſſes over to the claſs of productive expences, are ſo many *advances* returned in money, which in the courſe of the year reproduce 15*l.* net, and theſe 15*l.* conſtitute part of the reproduction of the landlord's rent for the year following; and by the remaining diſtribution of thoſe ſums, which return during the courſe of the ſame year to this ſame claſs, as it here appears from ſtep to ſtep, the total revenue is yearly reproduced.

THESE 15*l.* I ſay, which the landlord has poured back into the claſs of productive expences, are expended by the farmer, one half in the purchaſe of the productions furniſhed by his own claſs, ſuch as bread,

wine,

wine, meat, &c. the other half in apparel, furniture, tools, and the like, supplied by the clafs of barren expences.

THE 15*l.* of the landlord's rent which paffed over to the clafs of barren expences, are expended by the manufacturer, &c. half among the clafs of productive expences in bread, wine, and meat for his fubfiftence, and in the purchafe of raw materials to work upon, or to carry on for foreign commerce. The other half remains in the clafs of barren expences for his maintenance, and the reimburfement of his advances, that is to fay, of the fum juft now faid to be advanced by the manufacturer, till he can make up and difpofe of his goods.

THIS circulation, and this reciprocal and annual diftribution, proceed in the fame order by new fubdivifions to the laft farthing of the fums which pafs reciprocally from one clafs to another. Let us now examine the reflux, and total amount, of all thefe funds.

IT appears, by adding together the ſums carried to the claſs of barren expences, that the circulation carries 30*l.* to that claſs. Of theſe 30*l.* we muſt immediately deduct 15*l.* to replace the *annual advances*. There remain 15*l.* for wages. Thus we find, that the 15*l.* which immediately at firſt ſetting out paſs from the landlord's hands into the claſs of barren expences, replace in the ſaid claſs the 15*l.* annual advances; and that the wages of the ſaid barren claſs iſſue from another quarter, being the 15*l.* which this claſs receives from the claſs of productive expences.

THE produce of the claſs of productive expences is 60*l.* excluſive of the land-tax and tithes, and the intereſt on the primitive and annual advances; articles, which, not to render the order of expences too intricate, ſhall be taken notice of apart. The produce, I ſay, is 60*l.* to wit, 30*l.* which we have paid already into the hands of the landlord, and 30*l.* more, which conſtitute the reimburſement of the *annual advances*. Let us now trace the employment of theſe 60*l.*

WE ſaid, that the landlord bought 15*l.* worth of the land's produce, which is the ſame thing as if he received half his income in ſaid produce; 15 *l.* more paſs over to the claſs of barren expences, *viz.* 7*l.* 10*s.* which remain there of the firſt 30*l.* poured into by the landlord (for it appears that the barren claſs, by means of what it pours back at every ſtep to the productive claſs, retains but half of what it has received) and 7*l.* 10*s.* which it receives by the ſeveral returns made to it by the productive claſs. Of the remaining 30*l.* one half is conſumed or ſunk in the claſs of productive expences, by the men employed in raiſing the produce, and the amount of the other half goes to compleat the rent due to the landlord *.

The advances of the productive claſs reproduce every year themſelves and the income; and in like manner the income and theſe

* THE maintenance of cattle, though ſupplied by the produce of the earth, is not brought into this account, as the ſale of them forms in itſelf part of the income.

NOR are the reproductions of the 30*l.* advances taken any notice of, as they muſt be again beſtowed on the earth, to have a crop the next year.

these advances are every year consumed and reproduced: the advances likewise are consumed every year at the husbandman's; for they are nothing but the charges or expences which he is obliged to be at to reproduce them and the income, which is the net produce of the cultivation, after deducting all the charges attending it. If the advances, by being too weak, reproduced nothing but themselves, none but the husbandmen, and the members of the barren class, whose wares the husbandmen purchased, could subsist on the produce of the earth. In such circumstances, neither the state, nor the landlord, nor the church, could expect any thing without breaking in upon the subsistence of the husbandman, and those of the barren class, who supplied the husbandman with necessaries; without destroying the advances which are the means of reproducing the said subsistence; in short, without making a desart of the land. And then farewel to all husbandry, manufactures, and commerce!

IT is therefore necessary, in order to maintain the opulence, populousness, and power of a nation, that the husbandman's advances should be sufficient to obtain from the earth the greatest net produce, or greatest income possible; that is, that the productions should be in the greatest quantity, and of the greatest venal value possible. Besides, it imports every nation to maintain herself, by the venal value of the commodities of her own growth, in the most advantageous degree of opulence, relatively to the riches of the nations about her, and relatively to the reciprocal commerce which she carries on with them; for she would lose greatly by selling cheap, and buying dear, in her dealings with them. Such a commerce would redound entirely to their advantage, and would disturb the order of relative riches between her and her neighbours: a thing, which may easily happen by means of a bad police, by taxes, or, in a word, by any absurd regulations inverting the natural order of the nation's commerce.

BUT, to return to the 15*l.* allotted in the supposition of a net produce of *cent. per cent.* to the class of barren expences, to carry on that

that part of foreign commerce, which procures the vent of ſuch immediate fruits of the earth, as an agricole nation cannot conſume.

OF theſe 15*l.* one half, or 7*l.* 10*s.* are ſpent in purchaſing ſubſiſtence for the claſs itſelf; the other half is carried off by foreign commerce, which we refer to this ſame claſs. Thus an eighth of the whole amount of the productions enters foreign commerce in exportation, in raw materials, and in food for the manufacturers of the country, whoſe wares are exported to other nations. The trade, called reciprocal foreign commerce, conſiſts in the ſales of the merchant ballancing exactly the purchaſes made by him of the gold, ſilver, and other commodities, of the nation he deals with.

SUCH is the diſtributive order, in which the immediate productions of the earth are conſumed by the ſeveral claſſes, into which the inhabitants of an agricole country may be divided, and ſuch is the idea we ſhould form to ourſelves of the uſe and extent of foreign commerce in a flouriſhing agricole nation, whoſe government no way obſtructs the ſale of the immediate fruits of the earth. Thus in a nation, whoſe territory produces annually one hundred and twenty millions, the annual exportations would amount to fifteen millions. This may be conſidered as the genuine commerce of a well governed agricole nation, carried on in the immediate produce of its lands. This is the commerce which keeps up the vent and venal value of the immediate fruits of the earth, which makes agriculture flouriſh, renders all the lands of value, ſecures his revenue to the ſovereign, and his rent to the landlord, and is, at the ſame time, a certain ſource of wages for the hands employed in the claſs of barren expences.

SECTION

SECTION III.

The OECONOMICAL TABLE *considered relatively to Populousness.*

[See TABLE N° I.]

THE reciprocal vents, made by one class of expence to another, distributes on both sides the income of 30*l.* giving 15*l.* to each.

THE landlord subsists by the 30*l.* which he expends. The 15*l.* which he distributes to each class, added to the produce of the land-tax, the tithes, *&c.* annexed thereto, may subsist a man in each of the two other classes. Thus a rent of 30*l.* and its dependencies, may yield subsistence to three house-keepers.

ON this footing a rent of thirty millions is sufficient to yield subsistence to three millions of families, of four heads each.

WE ſaid, that the annual advances of the productive claſs, being nothing elſe but the diſburſements made for the reproductions, were repaid by the earth every year; we ſaid likewiſe, that half of theſe annual advances, *viz.* 15*l.* went to pay the wages of the hands employed by the farmer in the work of reproduction. Now theſe 15*l.* maintain another family; and as they ſtand for fifteen millions, we may reckon another million of families.

THUS then theſe forty-five millions, which, excluſive of the land-tax, tithes, intereſt of all the advances, both primitive and annual, would iſſue from year to year from the earth, would be ſufficient to yield ſubſiſtence to ſixteen millions of ſouls of every age, agreeable to this order of the circulation and diſtribution of the annual products and rents.

BY circulation, nothing more is meant here but the purchaſes made at the firſt hand, and paid for with the income which is divided between all the ſeveral claſſes of men, excluſive of commerce, which multi-

plies

plies ſales and purchaſes, without multiplying things, and is but a further increaſe of barren expences. Thus it appears, on the bare inſpection of the Table, that the pecuniary amount of the annual rents is ſufficient for circulation in the commerce of an agricole nation.

HERE then are ſixteen millions of ſouls ſubſiſted in a ſtate, in which the landlord's rents amount to thirty millions. But we have not as yet conſidered either the land-tax or the tithes, which, added to the landlord's rents, cannot fail of rendering very eaſy the circumſtances of thoſe ſixteen millions of ſouls, provided the population ſtops at this number, the beſt proportion to make a flouriſhing people; for the richer the agriculture of a nation, the fewer hands ſhe employs in raiſing corn, and the more ſhe ſtands in need of exportation to maintain plenty, and keep up the venal value of her productions. A flouriſhing nation, to enjoy her own annual riches, muſt buy from foreigners ſuch goods as her own lands don't produce. It is therefore requiſite that ſhe

ſhe ſhould ballance theſe purchaſes from foreigners by her ſales to them of the ſuperfluous part of her own produce. Without ſuch reciprocal commerce, her riches would in time dwindle to nothing; her productions would come to have no fixed or conſtant price; the annual returns of the huſbandman would become precarious; the incomes of the ſovereign, the landlord, and the church, would decreaſe, and the populouſneſs, kept up by theſe incomes, would be diminiſhed.

MANUFACTURES are very far from being, by the exportation of them, an infallible ſource of populouſneſs; they may be eſtabliſhed any where; they are itinerary, and inconſtant, in proportion to the force, with which neceſſity, or a proſpect of greater advantage, attracts them. A nation cannot reckon upon any riches as abſolutely her own, but the extent and fruitfulneſs of her lands. An agricole kingdom can build on nothing but a population maintained in eaſy circumſtances by the riches it draws from its own territory; and ſuch a population will be ſufficient to anſwer all the purpoſes that can be

ex-

expected from it, conformably to the ftate of the kingdom's riches.

IN calculating, how many inhabitants may be maintained in reafonably eafy circumftances, by this or any other amount of annual rents, we do not mean to limit or calculate the infinite number of flies who are always to be found about a rich hive; and which, without any infallible means of fubfiftence, are however maintained by the voluntary parfimony of the bees, and their own œconomy and refignation to put up with the leavings of others. A ftranger, who on entering my houfe, fees a fcullion attended by two fhoe-blacks at a time, muft not from thence conclude, that in rating the wages and perquifites of this fcullion, I have allowed fo much for this his vanity? By no means. I give myfelf no concern about it. No doubt he has his own reafons, fuch as they are, for acting in this manner; and thefe reafons, combined with an infinite number of fimilar reafons in the minds of others, yield a livelihood to fwarms of thefe officious and frugal flies called Savoyards. It is thus, that be-

besides the number of inhabitants secure of subsistence in a great state, there cannot but be a great number of others, who, attracted by the smell, croud about the pot, to suck up the scum of it. This portion of the inhabitants, however, will ever be relative to the produce, and as often as the produce falls short, it is, as it ought to be, the first portion that disappears.

WE shall see bye and bye how and why the land-tax must be reckoned half the landlord's income. Thus therefore, where the landlord's income amount to thirty millions, the land-tax must amount to fifteen millions*, and the tithes to seven millions five hundred thousand pounds. These two additions from a stock of twenty-two millions five hundred thousand pounds; and this sum, being an annual income distributed in the same direction with the income of the land-owners, must be divided into subsistence, and the means

* THESE fifteen millions, by being paid by the land, are raised without charges, and without any taxes upon persons or goods. France, well cultivated, could thus afford a land tax or impost of twenty-two millions and a half, and upwards, without hurting the national revenues, trade, or manufactures. 'Tis the only kind of impost that does not prove destructive in an agricole kingdom.

means of making their circumſtances more eaſy; for a proportionable number of inhabitants.

THE reimburſement of the annual advances,required by theſe two new portions of income, treated according to the rule heretofore deduced for the annual advances relative to the income of the land-owners, forms another ſtock of eleven millions, two hundred and fifty-thouſand pounds, which reunites with the diſtribution that extends to all the claſſes of inhabitants.

IF I have deviated from the hypotheſis, by which I confined myſelf to the conſideration of the landlord's income, excluſive of the land-tax and tithes, it was merely to compleat and purſue to the end the calculation of the ſtate s populouſneſs, all the while tacitly underſtanding theſe additions of ſubſiſtence. All to this, I ſtick to my firſt bounds.

THERE are therefore a million of landowners, whoſe expences are rated, one with another, at 30*l.* a head, and three millions of houſe-keepers, who ſubſiſt by labour, or lucrative employments. This makes, with the

the additions juſt now mentioned, 23*l.* 11*s.* for every head of a family of this claſs, as will appear hereafter by the total of the annual produce, which, in the preſent hypotheſis, yields, for the expences of the inhabitants, one hundred and ſix millions five hundred thouſand pounds, from which the perſonal expences of the land-owners muſt be deducted; the remainder belongs to the claſs ſubſiſting by labour or lucrative employments.

THE thirty millions income may be divided amongſt a ſmaller number of inhabitants. In this caſe, the fewer the land-owners, the more would the expence of their income exceed the conſumption which each of them could perſonally make; but then they would diſtribute a great deal in liberalities, or gather together other men to help them to conſume, what their income allowed them to expend: Thus theſe expences would be diſtributed pretty much in the ſame manner, as if there was a greater number of land-owners, each confined to a ſmaller expence. The ſame holds good of the inequality in the profits of thoſe belonging to the other claſſes, within which the advances, the intereſts, and the profits of of the farmers, merchants, and master-manufacturers, pass into the hands of the persons employed under them. These objects, by successive and reciprocal distributions, afford, in due gradation, profits or salaries, in their turn, to all the members of the lucrative professions. Hence the expences, even of the rich, are no more than a distributive transfer of expences, which extends to all the other inhabitants of a country, in proportion to their salaries.

SECTION IV.

The OECONOMICAL TABLE *considered relatively to the amount of the impost and tithes.*

[See TABLE, N° II.]

ONCE upon a time, in a certain nation, which as yet could barely bleat, but was very desirous of being able to articulate, there started up a wiseacre, who proposed to his countrymen a most wonderful project; this was, that every subject should give a halfpenny a day to the government, a contribution, which could not, he said, bear heavy upon any, even the poorest, member of the community, considering that there was not one amongst them, who did not already pay a great deal more upon what he consumed, &c. But, if this country was not, in matter of financial knowledge, *the kingdom of the blind*, at least it did not lie in a very distant latitude.

Every thing, or almoſt every thing there, went in impoſition; and nothing, or almoſt nothing, in impoſt.

But let me, before I go any farther, take notice of the ſignification I here attribute to theſe two words. By impoſition then, I mean the whole batch intended for the prince; and by impoſt, that portion of it which comes into his hands, clear of all the expences which attend the kneading of it.

To proceed. The above project was univerſally approved, in virtue of that general influence, which even the bare ſhadow of ſimplicity has over the minds of men. But it is an eaſy matter to ſee by our Table, that the calculation, in conſequence of which people may be ſuppoſed then to have ſaid, "The "king has twenty millions of ſubjects, for "example, men, women and children, and "a halfpenny a day for every one of them, "that is to ſay, two-pence a day for every "father of a family, poor or rich, makes "41,666*l.* 13*s.* 4*d.* a day, and 15,235,867*l.* "6*s.* 8*d.* a year." It is an eaſy matter, I ſay, to ſee, that this calculation ſuppoſed, as a cera certain fact, that it rained money upon the inhabitants, while they lay snoring in their beds, as it did manna upon the Israelites in the desart; for otherwise, all to the landlord, the subject, who earns nothing, can have nothing; and he who earns has nothing, but what he receives, as an agent or servant in the barren, or the productive class. If he is an agent in the productive class, he is, no doubt, considered as a proprietor, as far as his advances go; but by breaking in upon the interest of these advances, destined to make up the inevitable losses in husbandry, you'll soon break in upon the stock itself. Now lessening the stock, is lessening the reproduction, and of course the income; and lessening the income, is lessening the circulation of the whole state. If, on the contrary, he is only a servant or labourer, his salary, as being but just sufficient to afford him the necessaries of life, must be increased to the total amount of what is taken from him. Thus the blow given him re-acts upon the employer, from the employer on the advances, the reproductions, the incomes, and so makes the same round as in the first case.

IF, on the other hand, the contributor is agent or maſter in the barren claſs, the impoſt breaks in upon his advances, and he muſt, to reimburſe himſelf, raiſe the price of his commodities. Now, as he is paid for them by the landlord, on the one hand, and by the productive claſs on the other, this throws ſo much ſubſtance over to the barren claſs, as leſſens the reproduction in the ſame ratio, and diſturbs the march of the whole Table. If he is but ſervant in this ſame claſs, he is paid by, and is, as it were, a member of the employer, upon whom his overload bears, as in the productive claſs, and thence on the commodity, &c.

WE ſhall diſcuſs this kind of waſte in the Second Part, where we ſhall treat of the diſorder, which the Table may ſuffer by various phyſical and moral cauſes; what I now ſay of it, is merely to ſhew, at one glance, that, whatever ſhape the impoſt appears in, it is impoſſible it ſhould ariſe from any thing but the produce of the land; and that, unleſs it is immediately raiſed upon the net produce which conſtitutes the income, it loſes all ſtability and ſteadineſs. It loſes of its ſtrength

ſtrength by the number of its rebounds; of its amount by the difficulty of levying it, a circumſtance ſo favourable to monopoly; and of its certainty, by the ſmallneſs of the objects. There is, beſides, every moment, the greateſt danger of its degenerating into ſpoliation, and thus drying up its own ſources.

ACCORDINGLY, it is directly upon the income, or the net produce, that the author lays both impoſt and tithes. He omits them in his table, for fear of rendering it too complicate; though, after all, it is in appearance only that he omits them; for he makes thirty millions rent carry along with it fifteen millions impoſt, amounting, in the whole, to forty-five millions.

THE annual net produce of the land is conſidered apart from the annual reimburſements of the farmer. This net produce has three proprietors; the ſovereign, the landlord, and the church. The landlord can claim no more of the net produce, than the ſhare which he uſually receives, ſince it is according to the value of ſuch ſhare that he pays for the land. The other ſhares are un-

 alienable.

alienable. So that it is not the landlord, who pays either the tithes, or the uſual regular impoſt. Theſe portions of the ſubſtance do not belong to him. Thus, in ſhort, the regular impoſt is paid by nobody, but is ſupplied by the income of that part of the eſtate, which is the real patrimony of the public. Therefore the land-owner has no right to ſay, that it is his eſtate which pays the impoſt, when the impoſt is regular. Therefore the three proprietors juſt now mentioned have a common and lawful intereſt in the proſperity of agriculture, ſince they partake proportionably of the opulence it may create.

THIS proportion of the impoſt to the total net produce, will appear exceſſive to thoſe, who have never turned their thoughts this way. But, if they will juſt conſider the burthen of arbitrary impoſitions, whether ſuch as are perſonal, or ſuch as are deemed territorial; of the taxes on every kind of buſineſs, whether mercantile buſineſs, or law buſineſs, &c. eſpecially the exciſes on conſumption, on the tranſit of goods from one province to another, and on exportation and importation, &c. If they will read enough of of hiſtory to know, that there are ſome countries, not very near Monomotapa, where, in certain diſtricts, an acre under vines is found to yield 72 *l.* to the ſovereign, by the various taxes on the produce in all its involutions, and but 1 *l.* 10 *s.* clear of all charges to the owner. If, I ſay, ſuch perſons will but weigh all theſe exactions in a kingdom already ruined by them, and reflect that they tend to ruin the impoſt itſelf, it is impoſſible they ſhould not ſee, that the landlords would be very happy to purchaſe, at the expence even of half their income, an exemption from ſuch a complication of cankers.

IN the main, all the pretended riches, ariſing from ſuch exactions, are no better than an empty ſmoke; and, while from year to year they abſorb the fund, they gradually leſſen the produce, and annihilate all the reſources; they even come to nothing themſelves, as to the uſe to be made of them, by the indiſpenſable riſe they cauſe in the price of all the ſervices they are to purchaſe, as I ſhall demonſtrate, when I come to conſider the table in a conſumptive ſtate. But they do not bear the leſs upon the landlord's income, the enjoyment of which they annually deprive him of, and which they intercept at its very ſource, inſtead of waiting a little, till it has acquired ſome ſtrength in its progreſs; a miſtake by which the landlord is doubly a loſer.

A WORD therefore to the landlord. Your eſtate yields 1500*l.* of which you receive but 1250*l.* the remainder being kept by the farmer for the arbitrary taille, with which he is charged; and which both ruins him, and impairs your lands. Beſides this, you pay, in expending theſe 1250*l.* your ſhare of the impoſition laid upon mens wages, and upon commodities. Your farmer likewiſe labours under the ſame impoſition, which is again levied on the produce of your lands. All theſe impoſitions put together rob you of above 1000*l.* of the produce of your eſtate; and this produce, on account of the uncertain and unhappy condition of your farmer, does not amount to the fourth part of what it otherwiſe would.

BUT let us ſuppoſe all the chords broke, which hitherto entangled your farmer, and all

all the barriers levelled, which hindered his commodities from reaching, in all their immunity, the universal market in quest of a venal value. The net produce of your lands would then be fourfold, at least, what it is at present. The 1500*l.* would amount to 4500*l.* which, after paying a territorial impost of 2000*l.* instead of 250*l.* would turn out for your share 4000*l.* instead of 1000*l.* Your lands would be no longer exposed to those degradations, which continually threaten you with the total loss of your income; besides, you would get rid of the imposition, which, in your expences, swallows up one third of your income. Would you not have reason to think yourself very happy to give up forty to obtain a secure possession of eighty, instead of a very precarious possession of thirteen? This you think impossible; but have a little patience, and you shall see other details, which will remove all your doubts. Again; if, after calculating your profits arising from the productive class, you chuse to consider them with regard to the barren class, you will see, that on account of the great ease manufacturers must

acquire

acquire by an exemption from taxes, a rent of 4000*l.* would be equal to 7500*l.* as things now go, ſince you could afford to conſume three times as much. It is true, indeed, that you muſt conſume; for it is conſumption alone that can keep up a briſk circulation, according to the order of my table. But ſurely this cannot be called a grievance. Man ſeeks only to enjoy, and the only uſe he can make of riches is to enjoy them. We are deſirous to enjoy, I ſay, as ſoon as the natural order of things ceaſes to be inverted by any kind of injuſtice that may interfere with our enjoyment; and to be able to conſume a great deal, is to be rich: for, in this ſenſe, *conſumption* and *income* are ſynonimous terms.

LET us ſuppoſe, in fine, that the progreſſive contribution of one third of the income appears exorbitant; it cannot, however, be called ſpoliation *. And this is all the

* This progreſſion cannot be called exorbitant, as long as it is confined to its legal proportion, being the rightful patrimony of the Sovereign, whoſe income ſhould be proportionable to the opulence of his dominions. Beſides, no other perſon can claim a right to this third, when once ſet

the Author means; for he does not take upon him to judge of the political wants of a ſtate.

IN regard to tithes, the Author makes them amount to ſeven millions and an half, that is to ſay, one ſeventh of the total net income. It will perhaps be thought, that he has ſwelled this article too high, conſidering that no tithes are levied at this rate, or even that of one tenth; and that in many places they are but one twentieth or one thirtieth part of the produce. There are, beſides, ſeveral kinds of produce not ſubject to tithes, as woods, moſt meadows, &c. But then it muſt be conſidered, that tithes are now levied, not on the net produce, but on

ſet apart for his uſe. Moreover, as this encreaſe of opulence muſt depend on the goodneſs of the government, the benefits of it ſhould reach the throne. A community of intereſts herein between the Sovereign and ſubjects conſtitutes the ſecurity of ſociety. Sovereigns, as well as other men, are greedy of riches: beſides, they have more calls for riches than other men; and, therefore, ſhould be excited thereby to co-operate with their ſubjects for the common good. It would be bad policy to diſpute with them their ſhare in the encreaſe of riches to which they contribute. On the contrary, we ſhould this way awaken their attention, and endeavour to make them more watchful to ſecure both themſelves and us againſt domeſtic plunderers and foreign invaders.

on the total produce. Now, to meaſure the tithes by the total produce, we muſt have recourſe again to the rule laid down in our table.

WE have demonſtrated by the table, that the total produce amounts to 135*l.* 5*s.* to which, relatively to the tithes, muſt be added the very grain neceſſary for ſeed, calculated at 18*l.* 18*s.* All theſe ſums taken together conſtitute a titheable maſs of 154*l.* 3*s.* on half the produce of one plough; ſo that the tithe of 7*l.* 10*s.* is but the twentieth part of this total produce. This is nearly the proportion on an average, at which the tithe muſt be valued, in regard to corn, wine, cattle, &c. allowing for the other parts of the income, that are exempt from tithes; and it amounts to one fifteenth, or thereabouts, of the titheable produce. Now, if the tithe is found burdenſome on that footing, how much more burdenſome muſt it be, when levied on the total produce of a wretched cultivation, which hardly ever pays charges, nay often falls ſhort of them.

SECTION

SECTION V.

The OECONOMICAL TABLE *considered relatively to the National Cash.*

[See TABLE, N° II.]

MONEY, the idol of nations unacquainted with the genuine principles of political œconomy; money, which, when it has once gained an aſcendant, commits ſuch havock in both the moral and phyſical concerns of ſociety, is ſubject to the ſame rules with all other commodities; with this difference, that, as it ſcarcely has any uſual value of its own, it derives, more directly than any thing elſe, its venal value from the briſkneſs of commerce, which alone can beſtow upon it the quality of riches.

THE caſh of an agricole ſtate is nearly equal to the net produce, which it draws from its lands by means of commerce. Some perſons,

ſons, deſirous of forming to themſelves ideas of the caſh conſtantly remaining and circulating in the kingdom, tells us, with a great air of certainty: *By examining the books of the mint, the caſh coined ſince ſuch a period was found to amount to* 1700 *millions; of this ſo much was carried out of the kingdom by ſuch a war, and ſo much more by the preſent; in time of peace, we loſt ſo much a year by our commerce, which in ſo many years amounts to ſo much; therefore only ſo much remains.* Fine ſuppoſitions! We may as well pretend to calculate in this manner the number of ſwallows in ſpring.

WHEN we coin a great deal of money, it is a ſign that a great deal of our money finds its way out, and that it is of a juſter ſtandard than that coined elſewhere; or that foreign coin is allowed no currency among us, and that ours is allowed a currency in foreign countries, owing to the extraordinary goodneſs of it. But there is no more real coin in a kingdom than what circulates. What remains idle, is no better than a marcaſſite in a collection of natural curioſities,

as

as to its quality of an agent, which it thus renounces. In regard to its quality of riches, it is a commodity like any other commodity, all to this, that it takes up leſs room, and is not liable to corruption. It is, I ſay, a commodity which waits for a purchaſer.

Now, this commodity is not to be acquired by the ſtate, but by giving ſome other commodity in barter for it; and, as the ſtate, being poor, has no other commodity to give, (for if it was not poor, it would have no occaſion for money) it cannot obtain this money but in another way, called borrowing; that is to ſay, making a promiſe to return, giving ſecurity for the performance of this promiſe, and ſacrificing, from time to time, till the principle is paid, ſmall ſums of money to obtain the creditor's indulgence. This burdenſome bargain between the ſtate and private perſons, is ſo far from deſerving the name of reſource or finance, that it ought to be conſidered as the reverſe of both; ſince nothing deſerves the name of reſource, but what encreaſes the ſtrength of a ſtate; whereas this meaſure ſerves only

only to encreaſe its weakneſs; nothing deſerving the name of finance but the contribution of private perſons to the ſervice of the public; whereas this is a charge upon the public in favour of private perſons. This onerous bargain, I ſay, is ſo far from being a ſervice performed by an inhabitant and a ſubject, that as long as the ſtate continues to have any *credit*, that is to ſay, as long as people look upon the ſtate as able to perform its engagements, ſtrangers, and even enemies, will often lend it money on better terms than its uſurious citizens; and when the credit of the ſtate begins to totter, it is always the domeſtic creditor that gives notice of it to the foreign creditor.

THE money, therefore, that does not circulate, is of no manner of ſervice to the ſtate. With reſpect to that which circulates, and which alone deſerves the name of money in a ſtate, as it is but an intercalary equivalent between buyer and ſeller, it can only be in proportion to what it is to repreſent: the quantity, therefore, of money in any country will ever be proportionable to the

the quantity of production and consumption in the same, and no more.

IT appears by the table, that the 30*l.* paid the land-owner in money, are enough to keep up the circulation in the two classes of expences, between which these 30*l.* are distributed. Thus, in the given hypothesis, the total amount of the money is fixed at fifty millions; and it has been observed, that the national cash of England continues nearly at that proportion, which, in the present state of her riches, makes about 26,000,000*l.* sterling*. If England, therefore, has been obliged by her wars to contract immense debts, it is not because her subjects wanted money, but because her annual public expences exceeded, in time of war, her annual public revenues.

BUT tho' the subjects had money enough to supply the loans, the revenues would, nevertheless,

* The English themselves do not make it so much. One of their most celebrated writers upon trade has calculated, that the numerary value of the cash, necessary for circulation, is equal to one third of the yearly income of the lands. No doubt, he means the total income, which would bring it to a par, nearly, with the total net produce, or to about 25,000,000*l.* sterling.

theleſs, be, in time, overloaded with debts, and the nation undone, if the ſources of her revenues ſuffered ſuch a progreſſive waſte, as tended to leſſen the annual reproduction of riches.

IT is in this point of view that we are to conſider the ſtate of nations, becauſe money will be always ſpringing up afreſh in a nation, whoſe riches are always ſpringing up without any decay or interruption.

FOR about an age, that is to ſay, from 1450 to 1550, there was a great diminution in the quantity of money in Europe, as may be inferred from the price of commodities during that period; but this decreaſe of money ſignified nothing to the different nations of Europe, becauſe the venal value of this kind of riches was every where the ſame; and becauſe, with regard to money, their condition was the ſame, relatively to the income of their lands, which was every where equally meaſured by the uniform value of ſilver or money. In this caſe, it is much better, for the conveniency of mankind, that value ſhould ſupply the place of quantity,

tity, than quantity the place of value; at the ſame time that it is indifferent with reſpect to the riches of a nation, becauſe money in a nation forms but a ſmall object relatively to the total maſs of national riches, and is to be conſidered as riches, merely in proportion to its venal value, compared with the venal value of every other kind of riches.

PEOPLE are apt to think, that it is to the diſcovery of America Europe 'is indebted for her greater abundance of gold and ſilver; yet the value of money was fallen comparatively with that of other things, nearly to the foot at which we now ſee it, before the arrival of any American gold or ſilver in Europe. But theſe general truths make no alteration in the ſtate of the national caſh of any particular country, which will ever be proportionable to the income of the immovable eſtates, and the profits of foreign commerce.

IN the laſt age, under Lewis XIV. the ounce of coined ſilver was worth about 3 *s.* 1 *d.* $\frac{1}{2}$, Thus 95,400,000 ounces were then worth about 15,000,000 *l.* ſterling.

THIS was nearly the ſtate of the coin in France, at a time that ſhe was much richer than about the end of that monarch's reign.

THE general recoinage of 1716, did not amount to one fifth of that ſum. The ounce of coined ſilver went at that time for about 4*s.* 9*d.*½. This recoinage, therefore, ſcarce amounted to 50,000,000 ounces, which was more than one half leſs than the general recoinages of 1683 and 1693. Now, this ſtock of money cannot have increaſed by the annual coinages, ſince that period, but in proportion as the incomes of the nation have increaſed. How conſiderable ſoever theſe coinages may have been, they ſerved leſs to increaſe our ſtock of coined ſilver, than to replace what is annually carried out by contraband trade, by ſeveral branches of our paſſive commerce, and other uſes made of our money in foreign countries; for, by a fair calculation, theſe annual exports of coin, for the laſt forty-three years, might be ſhewn to amount to a very conſiderable ſum.

THE

THE augmentation of the nominal value of ſilver, which has for a long time ſtood at 5*s*. 9 *d*. is no proof that the quantity of the national caſh has much increaſed. On the contrary, we may infer from thence, that it has leſſened, ſince the nominal value was increaſed, merely to ſupply the place of reality with appearances.

THESE eſtimates agree but little with the vulgar notions concerning the quantity of a country's national caſh. The common people make the riches of a ſtate conſiſt in money; but money, like all other productions, is riches, as has been already obſerved, merely in proportion to its venal value, and may be as eaſily acquired than any other commodity, by paying for it with ſome other kind of riches. Its quantity in every ſtate is in proportion to the uſe made of it, which uſe is greater or leſs, according to the amount of the annual ſales and purchaſes in ſaid ſtate; and the amount of theſe ſales and purchaſes will be greater or leſs, according to the amount of the ſtate's incomes. Moreover, money is not to be purchaſed, but by other kinds of riches; and, therefore, a nation muſt be rich to purchaſe it; ſo that the acquiſition of money does not add to the riches of him who pays for it; and he cannot enjoy the uſe of this kind of riches, but by ſelling it, in his turn, for ſome other kind of commodity.

THE coin of a nation, therefore, ſhould ever be in proportion to the amount of its incomes. A greater ſtock would be uſeleſs. The nation would ſoon exchange its ſuperfluity with other nations, for ſome other kind of riches more beneficial, or more agreeable; for monied men, even the moſt ſaving, are always upon the watch to make ſome advantage of their pelf. Their finding opportunities to lend it in a country at a high intereſt, is a ſure ſign, that in ſuch country it is, at moſt, in the proportion we have obſerved, ſince the inhabitants pay ſo dear for the uſe of it.

SECTION VI.

The OECONOMICAL TABLE *considered in the estimation of the produce, and capital stock of every kind of riches.*

[See TABLE, N° II.]

I AM now going to make an estimate of an agricole, or landed nation's riches of every kind, in that state of its incomes here assumed by us. This estimate is very far from being imaginary, and I thought it necessary to give my readers a detail of it, the better to remove those prejudices, which make all the riches of a nation consist in money. Here we may see the real amount of the nominal value necessary to realize, in point of bargain-making, and put in motion, by means of barter, the general mass of riches; and it will appear to make but the fifty-fifth part of such general mass. Of this a ſingle glance at the table might have been ſufficient to convince the reader; but it is impoſſible to diſplay, in too many lights, ſuch fundamental principles, as tend to contradict and deſtroy common prejudices.

THOSE, who hate figures, will be ſcared by this article; and of thoſe, who do not hate them, ſuch as would gladly loſe themſelves in the ſuppoſed immenſity of the funds and reſources of a great ſtate, tho' merely to make, on every occaſion, a bad uſe of ſuch a ſuppoſition, and love to buoy themſelves up with the chimerical multiplicity of the incomes, ſquandered by the lazy and luxurious members of an uſurious ſtate, will be apt to think, that it is confining their ideas to take from them their gilded proſpect of infinity.

OTHERS (and they are the greateſt number) accuſtomed to the petty calculations of the riches about them, will think they ſee billions drop out of the clouds. But all this is nothing to the calculator. It is for the uſe of men of ſenſe alone, that he has undertaken the taſk. Thoſe, who apply themſelves to the ſtudy of ſuch ſciences as are moſt uſeful to mankind,

are

are not so few as people generally imagine; and they never fail, in the end, to bring over the rest of mankind to their own way of thinking.

Riches of the class of productive expences.

I SAID, that lands yielding an income of 30,000,000 *l.* to the land-owner, yielded, besides, an impost of 15,000,000 *l.* and tithes to the amount of 7,500,000 *l.* amounting in the whole to 52,500,000 *l.* To this let us add the reproduction of the annual advances, amounting to 52,500,000 *l.* and interest, at ten per cent. for these advances, the whole making

110,250,000 *l.*

IN a country full of vineyards, meadows, woods, &c. but about two-thirds of said sum would be the produce of the plough. This portion, in a thriving state of great culture, performed by stout horses, would require 333,334 ploughs, at 120 acres to a plough, an equal number of men to drive them, and 40,000,000 of acres.

IN

IN France, 275 millions ſterling, inveſted in advances, would be ſufficient to extend this kind of culture to 60 millions of acres.

WE ſaid before, (p. 25.) that the primitive advances, requiſite to ſet a plough completely agoing in the great culture, or the firſt expence to ſtock the land with cattle, inſtruments, ſeed, ſubſiſtence, wages, &c. in the courſe of two years labour before the firſt crop, might be valued at 500*l.* Thus the primitive advances, requiſite for 333,334 ploughs, make - - - 166,667,000*l.*

To this ſum muſt be added the intereſt of theſe advances, which ought to yield 10 per cent. at the loweſt, conſidering that the fruits of the earth are liable to accidents, which every ten years run away with one year's crop at leaſt. Beſides, the machines, &c. purchaſed by theſe advances, muſt be frequently repaired and recruited: on this foot, therefore, the intereſt of the primitive advances, requiſite for the eſtabliſhment of the farmers, muſt amount to 16,666,700*l.*

MEADOWS,

MEADOWS, vineyards, gardens, and woods, cost the farmer but few primitive advances. The value, therefore, of these primitive advances, along with those of the land-owner in plantations, and other works usually performed by him, may be reduced to

50,000,000*l.*

IT is true, indeed, that vineyards and gardens require very great annual advances; however, considered relatively to the annual advances requisite for the other branches of country-business, they may, on a medium, be comprehended in the total of the annual expences already laid down.

THUS, the total annual reproduction in net produce, in annual advances, and interest on them and the primitive advances, valued according to the order of the table, make - - - 126,916,700*l.*

GREAT as this sum may appear, the lands of France might, by means of proper advances and free markets, be made to produce a much greater.

OF

OF this ſum of 126,916,700*l.* we are to allow 26,250,000*l.* being half the reproduction of the annual advances, for the maintenance of cattle, ſo that there remains (allowing that the whole impoſt returns into the circulation, and does not eat in upon the huſbandman's advances) 100,666,700*l.* for the annual expences of the men.

Eſtimate of the ſtock of productive riches.

WE are firſt to put down the primitive advances requiſite to ſet the ploughs agoing, which advances have been already rated at 166,667,000*l.*

THE primitive advances for meadows, fiſh-ponds, woods, vineyards, gardens, &c. already rated at - - 50,000,000*l.*

I make no ſeparate eſtimate of the value and produce of cattle, as I included them in the advances of the farmers, and in the total of the annual products. But I ſhall eſtimate the lands, becauſe, relatively to their venal value, they may, in ſome ſort, be be confidered as moveable riches, in as much as their price is affected by the variations in the price of the other kinds of riches neceffary to cultivate them. In fact, lands are fubject to decay, and the owners cannot but fuffer in the venal value of them, in proportion to the lofs of the farmers by fuch decay.

THE lands, which annually produce for man's immediate benefit, 100,666,700*l.* of which 52,500,000*l.* are net produce, valued at thirty years purchafe, conftitute, in this point of view, a treafure amounting to

1,575,000,000*l.*

Total of the funds of the productive clafs,

1,791,667,000*l.*

BY adding to this fum the 126,916,700*l.* arifing from the annual produce, as deduced in the preceeding cafe, it will appear, that the total amount, charges included, of the riches of the productive clafs is

1,918,583,700*l.*

Eftimate

Estimate of the riches of the barren class.

THIS class, it is known, produces nothing; consequently, we are to estimate nothing but what it may be actually possessed of.

Now the riches this class is actually possessed of, according to the proportions laid down in the table, are,

1st, The fund of annual advances 26,250,000*l.*

2dly, The primitive advances for the establishment of manufactures, construction of instruments, machines, mills, forges, &c. - - - 100,000,000*l.*

3dly, The coin or money computed by us at - - - 50,000,000*l.*

4thly, The value of four millions of houses, or lodgings, for four millions of families, reckoning each house, one with another, at 3*l.* 15*s.* a year * - 300,000,000*l.*

5thly,

* He values them at twenty years purchase. The houses in France are generally stronger than those in England.

5thly, The value of the common furniture of the said houses, computed, one with another, at a year's income or gain of four millions of heads of families,

100,000,000*l.*

6thly, The value of the gold and silver plate, toys, precious stones, looking-glasses, pictures, books, and other lasting works of the handicraftsman, which descend from one generation to another; this, in the state of opulence, in which we here suppose a nation, may amount to

100,000,000*l.*

7thly, The value of the ships of war, merchant-ships, arsenals, &c. supposing it to be a maritime state; likewise, that of artillery and other durable warlike stores, and of durable buildings for use or ornament, which are riches merely in proportion to the riches they cost; all these objects may be rated together at

150,000,000*l.*

I omit the necessaries of life, and other commodities, stored up in shops and merchants

chants warehouſes for annual uſe or conſumption, whether produced or made up at home, or imported from abroad; and likewiſe ſuch goods as are intended for exportation, becauſe they are all contained in the ſtate of annual productions and expences, conformably to the order exhibited in the table.

TOTAL amount of the riches belonging to the claſs of barren expences

826,250,000*l.*

By adding to which the

TOTAL amount of the riches belonging to the claſs of productive expences

1,918,583,700*l.*

THE general maſs of riches, belonging to a flouriſhing landed nation, will, in the given hypotheſis, appear to amount to about

2,744,833,700*l.*

WE here ſpeak of an opulent nation, poſſeſſed of a territory and of advances, which yield annually, and without decay, a net produce

produce of 52,500,000*l.* for its annual consumption. But these riches, especially the value of lands, being upheld from year to year by nothing but the annual produce, may utterly perish, or, at least, come to lose great part of their value, in an ill governed agricole state; and this declension may in a very short time be very considerable, through the want of freedom of commerce in the immediate fruits of the earth, and through the annihilation of the advances upon which the reproduction of them depends.

Noli me tangere! is the motto of these advances.

SECTION VII.

The OECONOMICAL TABLE *considered in the conditions necessary to the free play and prosperity of the political machine.*

[See TABLE, N° II.]

IT appears by the foregoing Table, that in a regular and uninterrupted circulation of an annual income of 52,500,000 *l.* an equal sum, which returns into the circulation, restores yearly to the productive class the advances requisite for the reproduction of the same income, and the same advances; wherefore, the continuation of this reproduction supposes,

1st, THAT every farthing of the said 52,500,000*l.* income, enters the annual circulation, and runs through it in its whole extent; that no money is hoarded up, or, at least, that as much money is returned in-

 to

to the circulation by ſome hands, as is taken from it by others; otherwiſe the pecuniary fortunes thus amaſſed, would prove ſo many obſtructions in the courſe of part of theſe annual incomes of the nation, keep back the national caſh, and thereby impede the return of the huſbandman's advances, the payment of the handicraft's wages, and the conſumption by the different claſſes of men who belong to the lucrative profeſſions. This obſtruction of the national caſh would leſſen the reproduction of the income, and the impoſt.

2dly, THAT no part of the income is exported without an adequate return in money or goods.

3dly, THAT the nation loſes nothing by its foreign commerce, which may very well happen, notwithſtanding the great profits made by private traders, in ſelling the goods imported by them to their fellow-ſubjects. Nay, every profit of this kind is ſo much taken from the circulation of the net produce of the land, and ſuch a defalcation cannot but

but be extremely prejudicial to both diſtribution and reproduction.

4thly, THAT the ballance of the gold and ſilver paſſing and repaſſing between the nation and foreigners, is not made the ſtandard of their commerce, without examining what profit ariſes from the goods themſelves, which have been bought or ſold; for it often happens, that the nation, which receives a ſurplus in money, is the loſer; and this loſs affects the reproduction and diſtribution of the incomes. In a foreign trade, where the immediate fruits of the earth are exchanged for handicraft works, the diſadvantage is generally on the ſide of the nation that purchaſes the firſt, becauſe there is a great deal more profit to be had in ſelling them, than in ſelling the latter.

5thly, THAT the land-owners, and ſuch as belong to the lucrative profeſſions, do not ſuffer themſelves to be betrayed by any uneaſineſs, which the government might not foreſee, time enough to prevent it, into a barren parſimony, capable of hindering any part of their incomes, or gains, from being properly circulated and diſtributed.

6thly, THAT the adminiſtration of the finances affords no opportunity to thoſe concerned in the receipt or diſburſement of them, to amaſs pecuniary fortunes, and thereby divert a portion of the public revenues, from the grand operations of circulation, diſtribution, and reproduction.

7thly, THAT the impoſt is neither deſtructive of, or diſproportioned to, the maſs of the national incomes; that the augmentations of it keep pace with the augmentations of the ſaid maſs; that it bears directly on the net produce of the earth, and by no means on commodities of any kind; as, in the latter caſe, the charges of perception would be multiplied, commerce injured, and part of the national riches annually deſtroyed. Likewiſe, that the impoſt is not levied on the advances of the farmer; for theſe advances ſhould be conſidered as ſo many immoveable goods, which ought to be moſt ſcrupulouſly preſerved for the production of both impoſt

impoſt and income. Without this precaution, the impoſt becomes ſpoliation, and cauſes a decay, which muſt, ſooner or later, infallibly end in the deſtruction of the ſtate.

8thly, THAT the primitive and annual advances of the farmer, are ſufficient to make the earth yearly reproduce, at the leaſt, double the latter, and 10 *per cent.* upon both. Where either of the two kinds of advance are leſs than they ought to be, the expences of agriculture will not only afford a ſmaller net produce, but be much heavier in proportion to it.

9thly, THAT the children of the farmers, by ſettling in the country, perpetuate a race of huſbandmen; for when any vexations oblige them to deſert their fields, and take ſhelter in towns, they carry along with them the riches of their family, heretofore employed in agriculture. It is not ſo much men, as riches, that ought to be invited into the country; for the more riches are employed in the production of corn, the fewer hands it requires, the better it thrives, and the more clear profit it yields. Such is the great culture of rich farmers compared with the petty culture of poor cottagers, who make use of cows or bullocks.

10thly, THAT care is taken to prevent the emigration of the inhabitants, who would employ their riches in other countries.

11thly, THAT the exportation of the immediate fruits of the earth is no way obstructed, *for the reproduction of a thing will ever be as the demand for it.*

12thly, THAT nothing is done, which may lower the price of the immediate fruits of the earth, or any other kind of commodities within the kingdom; for this would render the trade with foreigners prejudicial to the kingdom. WHATEVER THE VENAL VALUE IS, SUCH WILL THE INCOMES BE. PLENTY AND CHEAPNESS DO NOT CONSTITUTE RICHES. SCARCITY AND DEARNESS ARE THE PARENTS OF MISERY. PLENTY AND DEARNESS CONSTITUTE OPULENCE.

13thly,

13thly, THAT the cheapneſs of neceſſaries are not conſidered as of any real ſervice to the inferior claſſes of people; it lowers their wages; renders their life leſs comfortable, affords them leſs work, and lucrative employment; and reduces the rent of lands.

14thly, THAT the common people are not debarred the means of living at their eaſe, for otherwiſe they could not ſufficiently contribute to the conſumption of ſuch neceſſaries as muſt be conſumed at home, by which, of courſe, the reproduction and incomes of the nation would infallibly ſuffer.

15thly, THAT the multiplication of cattle is encouraged; for it is by cattle that the land is ſupplied with the manures neceſſary to yield rich crops.

16thly, THAT the luxury of decoration is not ſolicited, becauſe this kind of luxury ſubſiſts entirely at the expence of the luxury of ſubſiſtence, which is that kind of luxury that keeps up the price, and the demand for the immediate fruits of the earth, and upholds

upholds the reproduction of the nation's incomes.

17thly, THAT the government does not favour any thing but the productive expences, and the exportation of the immediate fruits of the earth, leaving the barren expences entirely to themselves.

18thly, THAT, in the extraordinary exigencies of the state, no resources are expected, but from the prosperity of the subjects; and, by no means, from the credit of the financiers; *for pecuniary fortunes are clandestine fortunes, which know neither king nor country.*

19thly, THAT the government avoids such loans, as encumber the public revenue with heavy debts and a heavy interest; and are, consequently, attended with a trade in the finances, by means of transferrable papers, the interest upon which is constantly increasing the barren pecuniary fortunes. These fortunes cause a divorce, as it were, between the finances of the state and agriculture, and so rob the latter of the riches requisite to improve and cultivate the earth.

20thly,

20thly, THAT the nation, which has a great extent of country to cultivate, and the means of carrying on a great foreign trade in the immediate fruits of its lands, does not apply too much money, and too many hands, to manufactures, and the commerce of luxuries, to the prejudice of her husbandry works and expences; for such a kingdom ought, above all things, to be well stocked with rich husbandmen.

21stly, THAT the lands employed in raising corn, are united as much as possible, so as to form large farms carried on by rich husbandmen; for large farms require less expence of every kind, and at the same time yield a greater net produce, in proportion, than small ones. Small farms employ to no purpose, and at the expence of the land's produce, a greater number of poor families, who have too little land and stock to carry on a rich culture. Such a multiplicity of farmers tends less to increase the number of inhabitants, than an augmentation of the incomes would do; for the most certain populousness, and the most applicable to all the different occupations, by which mankind is is divided into different classes, is that, which is kept up by the net produce of the land. Every profitable saving in those works, which may be carried on by means of animals, machines, rivers, &c. tends to the increase of populousness, and the advantage of the state, because the greater the net produce of agriculture, the better wages and profits can be afforded for other services and works.

22dly, THAT every man is at liberty to employ his field in the production of whatever his interest, his stock, and the quality of the ground points out to him, as capable of yielding the greatest profit. No favour should be shewn to monopoly in the cultivation of the earth; for it would prove detrimental to the general income of the nation. Those governments, which favour the production of commodities of the first want, more than the production of those of the second, to the lessening the venal value of both, act through narrow views, which do not take in the effects of foreign trade, that supplies all deficiencies, and settles the price of those goods, which every nation can raise

to

to the greateſt advantage. The immediate produce of the earth, and the impoſt, are, in every ſtate, the riches of the firſt neceſſity to defend it againſt ſcarcity and invaſion, to maintain the glory and power of the ſovevereign, and promote the proſperity of the ſubjects.

23dly, THAT the government thinks leſs of ſaving money, than of forwarding the operations eſſential to the kingdom's proſperity; for the heavieſt expences may be rendered light by a proportionable increaſe of riches. But profuſion muſt not be confounded with expence. Practices, that deſerve the name of profuſion, might ſoon ſwallow up all the riches of both prince and people.

24thly, THAT leſs attention is beſtowed on the multiplication of the people, than on the increaſe of their riches. A moderate number of inhabitants, living in eaſy circumſtances, created by plentiful incomes, is far preferable to a greater number pinched thro' any deficiency in them. Beſides, eaſy circumſtances afford more reſources in exigencies

gencies of the ſtate, than great numbers, and, at all times, better means of making agriculture flouriſh.

WITHOUT theſe conditions agriculture, which the table ſuppoſes to yield the ſame produce, as in England, would be a mere bubble. But the principles of it are not the leſs certain, nor leſs the genuine principles of the ſcience of œconomical government; by which we do not here mean that trivial ſcience, which has no other object but the caſh and finances of a kingdom, and the motion of its money, by a traffic of money, in which the charms of credit and intereſt, &c. produce merely, as at gaming, a barren circulation. It is only in a compleat knowledge of the true ſources of riches, and of the means of multiplying and perpetuating them, that the ſcience of the œconomical government of a kingdom can be ſaid to conſiſt.

AN œconomical government unlocks the ſources of riches; riches attract men; men and riches make agriculture flouriſh, extend commerce, give life to induſtry, increaſe and

and perpetuate riches. An œconomical government guards againſt any decay in the opulence and ſtrength of a nation. On theſe plentiful reſources depend the ſucceſs of every other branch of the adminiſtration of a kingdom. An œconomical government confirms the power of a ſtate, procures it the conſideration of other ſtates, ſecures the glory of the prince, and the happineſs of the people. The views of an œconomical government take in all the eſſential principles of a perfect government, in which authority is ever ready to protect and do good; ever watchful, and of courſe ever reſpectable. It is incapable of committing miſtakes; it cannot give any umbrage; it every where ſupports the intereſts of the nation, good order, public right, the power and dominion of the ſovereign.

EXPLA-

THE

OECONOMICAL TABLE.

PART II.

SECTION I.

The OECONOMICAL TABLE *considered in its private Depredations.*

[See TABLE, N° III.]

Excess of LUXURY.

LET us now study the Oeconomical Table in a state of disorder. We shall consider it in this respect, but in seven distinct points of view. 1st. In its private depredations; that is to say, in the disorders which

 proceed

proceed from the immorality and ignorance of a nation. The ſix other aſpects are public depredations, viz. 2dly, Relatively to the ſpoliation of the productive advances; 3dly, Relatively to population; 4thly, Relatively to the coin; 5thly, Relatively to the police; 6thly, Relatively to commerce; 7thly, in fine, Relatively to deſtructive impoſts.

To judge rightly, immorality and ignorance always proceed from ſome public error. But though it is part of my buſineſs to trace to, and correct from, the very roots, phyſical miſcalculations, I am not bound to attack, in the ſame ſenſe, moral prejudices. When, therefore, I mention the word *Luxury*, it is not to be expected I ſhould throw out againſt it that abundance of arguments naturally ſuggeſted by the bare mention of the word, to every patriot heart. In this place I only ſpeak of phyſical luxury.

IN the new plate now before us, the Table has loſt its equilibrium. Our buſineſs is to diſcover and explain the cauſes and the effects of this diſorder. By the firſt lines of our explanation of the Table, it appears, that the diſtri-

distribution of the church, king, and landlord's income, is what puts in motion the machine of circulation. It is obvious, that more of these expences may fall to one side than to the other, as he who makes them indulges himself more or less in the luxury of subsistence, or that of decoration, which last alone, properly speaking, deserves that appellation.

WE have heretofore assumed, in the Oeconomical Table, a mean state of things, in which the reproductive expences yield from year to year the same income; but we may easily form a judgment of the alterations that would ensue in the annual reproduction, according as the reproductive, or barren expences, get the start of each other; this, I say, we may easily form a judgment of, by the alterations that would ensue in the Table.

IT is in this state of things that we here exhibit it. We suppose, that the land-owner, &c.'s luxury of decoration has increased one sixth; that is to say, that they pay 4 *l.* 7 *s.* 6 *d.* more, than they did before, to the class of barren expences, so as to make the whole of what they bestow upon it

30*l.* 12*s.* 6*d.* and reduce what they beſtow upon the claſs of reproductive expences to 21*l.* 17*s.* 6*d.* Such is the power of example, that manners ſoon circulate through all the claſſes of ſociety; the moral concatenation being every where the ſame with the phyſical. This miſapplication of one ſixth will be the ſame with the handicraftſman and the huſbandman; and the conſequence will be, that by carrying on the Table, according to this new arrangement, it will appear at bottom thereof, that the reproduction of the total income of 52*l.* 10*s.* which includes rent, tithes, and land-tax, is reduced to 45*l.* 15*s.* and the reimburſements of the huſbandman, amounting before to 82*l.* 15*s.* are reduced to 72*l.* 2*s.* The total deficiency, therefore, amounts to 17*l.* 8*s.* ſo that the loſs, on this occaſion, is about two-fifths.

IF, on the contrary, the king, church, and land-owner, increaſe in the ſame degree their expence in the conſumption or exportation of the immediate fruits of the earth, the reproduction of an income of 52*l.* 10*s.* would amount to 57*l.* 6*s.* and the huſbandman's returns amounting before to 82*l.* 15*s.* would now

now amount to 90*l.* 6*s.* which is an increaſe of 7*l.* 11*s.* Thus the total increaſe would be 12*l.* 7*s.* or about one tenth, and would continue at this rate as long, as the land and the labour of the huſbandmen could contribute to it.

SUCH are the effects of a conſtant and uniform raiſing of the price of commodities of the firſt neceſſity; and thus we ſee how the wiſeacres, who do all they can to keep theſe commodities at a cheap rate, labour, without knowing it, to deſtroy the incomes and ſubſiſtence of a nation.

IT appears likewiſe, by this very ſimple demonſtration, that an exceſs in the luxuries of decoration may alone very ſpeedily ruin the moſt opulent nation. It further appears, of what importance it is to ſupport opulence in theſe different orders of a ſtate, which, according to the common cuſtoms of ſociety, may employ their ſuperfluities in the luxuries of ſubſiſtence; the obſcure rich being, as it were, forced by the prejudices of ſociety to launch into the luxuries of decoration, and kept from thoſe of ſubſiſtence, which, at preſent, would ſit ill upon them, and only ſerve to render them ridiculous.

We may likewiſe gueſs how little the œconomical ſcience was underſtood in that country, wherein they conſidered, as a tax upon luxury, a tax upon ſervants and upon horſes, which conſume ſo much corn, forage, and other commodities of the productive claſs.

It is therefore falſe, that all kinds of expence are indifferent.

What we have been juſt now obſerving, in regard to the capital expences in the immediate fruits of the earth, all of which yield plentiful returns in an agricole kingdom, is by no means applicable to little trafficking ſtates that have no territory.

Such ſtates cannot ſtint themſelves too much in any kind of expence, as it is by means of parſimony alone, that they can hope to preſerve and increaſe the ſtock of riches requiſite for their commerce, and likewiſe afford to trade at leſs expence than other nations, ſo as to ſecure to themſelves a preference at foreign markets. But as to the great landed powers, it is impoſſible they ſhould thrive, as long as they indiſcriminately attribute

tribute their poverty to every kind of expence. It is not to expence itſelf, but to the peculiar nature of it, that their poverty is to be attributed, as we have already proved; it is to the inequality of the repayments, &c. and ſtill more to the œconomical arrangements of police, finance, and commerce. This we ſhall ſoon examine, after treating curſorily of ſome errors of detail concerning agriculture.

IN what does the proſperity of a landed nation conſiſt? IN PLENTIFUL ADVANCES, TO PERPETUATE AND INCREASE THE NET PRODUCE OF THE EARTH; IN A FREE AND EASY DOMESTIC AND FOREIGN COMMERCE; IN THE ENJOYMENT OF THE ANNUAL RETURNS OF THE REAL ESTATES; IN PECUNIARY AND READY PAYMENTS OF LAND-RENTS AND THE LAND-TAX.

A PLENTY of productions is obtained by plentiful advances. Conſumption and commerce keep up the demand for, and the venal value of the productions. The venal value is the meaſure of national riches. Theſe riches are a ſtandard for the tribute which is imposed upon them, and bring in the money which is to pay the said tribute, and which ought to circulate in commerce, but never superabound in a country. Such superabundance would lessen the use and consumption of the annual productions, which are to perpetuate real genuine riches in the state, by reproduction, and a reciprocal commerce.

PEOPLE had better notions than we have, concerning the nature and source of true riches, at that period, wherein history has thought proper to celebrate the procession, with which the inhabitants of *Goodman's-Chester*, in *England*, went to welcome their monarch. They drove one hundred and eighty ploughs to meet him. This was a retinue truly worthy of a king. The bees, so faithful, so obedient, and so affectionate to their queen, never offer her any thing but their sweetest honey. To offer princes a voluntary tribute, and a free gift, is both the duty and the happiness of subjects; but to present them with implements of husbandry, as fructifying under their protection, is to lay before them, at once, the proofs of our gratitude,

titude, the buttresses of their power, and the pledges of our love. It is acknowledging them for the true shepherds of mankind.

RICH husbandmen, and rich country merchants, are the pillars of landed and independent states.

IN the great culture, a single man drives a plough drawn by two horses, and this plough does as much work as three ploughs drawn by two bullocks each, and driven by six men. In the last case, for want of the primitive advances requisite to establish the great culture, the annual expences are immense in proportion to the net produce, which is, in a manner, next to nothing. Besides, this petty culture requires ten or twelve times more land to yield the same net produce. What is worse, when the land-owners cannot meet with farmers substantial enough to bear the expences of a good culture, the advances, such as they are, are made at the expence of the land itself. The produce of the meadows is devoured in winter by the bullocks employed in cultivating it, and a portion of the land must be given up to them to graze upon in summer; the net produce of the crop is so insignificant,

significant, that the leaſt increaſe in the impoſt is ſufficient to make all the parties concerned renounce ſuch poor remains of tillage; a thing, which has happened in many places, merely through the wretched indigence of the inhabitants.

THIS detail of agriculture will, I know, in many places, meet with oppoſition, from cuſtom and local prejudices. The men of any fortune in the poor provinces, in which one third of the arable lands lyes uncultivated, and almoſt all the reſt are reduced to the petty culture here complained of; theſe men, I ſay, will affirm, that the great culture is not proper for their ſoil, as being too heavy, or too light, for ſo impatient an animal as an horſe; that it coſts them little or nothing to feed their oxen all the ſummer, by letting them run on the commons, and other open grounds; that oxen require neither oats nor barley, nor ſhoes, nor expenſive harneſs; and a thouſand other things. But theſe are only ſo many arguments of a methodical wretchedneſs.

To be convinced of this, we need only conſider a ſubſtantial farmer, ſuch as may be found

found in some provinces of the kingdom; and see if this man, whose every thought, every step, every action, every sinew, in fine, is continually bent upon some decent profit, and consequently upon the improvement of his farm; if this man, I say, is any way sparing in his primitive or annual advances? Are not his horses the strongest and the dearest, and withal the best kept, of the whole country? Are not his servants the best paid, and the best fed and cloathed, &c. This man, without ever seeing our Table, hits the mark by the mere dint of experience, and knows that his endeavours must prosper in proportion to the good order in which he keeps his servants, his cattle, &c. agreeable to the proverb; *Poor men, poor work*, and to what our Table teaches; *the more is laid out upon land, the more will it yield.*

How comes it then, that so many consider, as a piece of œconomy, every saving in point of forage, harness, &c. Why, because neither they, nor those who were the first to pursue the same method, ever had the stock necessary to establish any other that required larger advances, and was of course capable of yielding larger returns; because the rich men

men among them knew ſo little from whence they derived their riches, that they always found ſome employment or another for their ſuperfluity, beſides that of contributing to the grand work of reproduction.

To prove that a more expenſive method would be more profitable, ſuppoſe your heaths, and other open grounds, converted into good meadows, yielding a double crop of hay, or well ploughed, and then ſown with the moſt beneficial kind of corn; ſuppoſe the forage produced by this management conſumed at night near your lay-ſtalls, by your black cattle, or ſheep, or by ſtout horſes, that would do three times as much work as the ſame number of oxen, and who, beſides, require no ſubſiſtence but what is the produce of their own labour.

SUPPOSE, moreover, your lands never obliged to lie fallow to recover themſelves, but yielding every year the beſt of corn and forage. This is no chimerical ſuppoſition; for this kind of agriculture flouriſhes among your neighbours, in a leſs favourable climate. Nay, we may ſtill find ſome examples of it at home, in the neighbourhood of the

ca-

capital; and it is upon theſe examples, that this table has been conſtructed. By fancying ourſelves in this flouriſhing country, and looking a little about us, we may be enabled to form ſome judgment of our preſent parſimony, or rather indigence.

THE rich farmer covers his fields with cattle, and by that means obtains thoſe manures which yield rich crops. This is a new ſpecies of riches, and the moſt profitable of all riches.

THIS advantage is to be obtained by the ſale, the working up, and the wearing of our own wool within the kingdom; by the great conſumption of meat, milk, butter, cheeſe, &c. but, above all things, in an opulent nation, by the conſumption of the common people, who are the moſt numerous part of it; for it is merely in proportion to ſuch conſumption, that the demand for cattle can increaſe, and cattle, of courſe, be multiplied; a circumſtance upon which the obtaining of plentiful crops eſſentially depends.

THIS plenty of corn and cattle prevents all apprehenſions of famine in a kingdom ſo

fertile

fertile in the primary means of ſubſiſtence. The food, yielded by cattle in ſuch a kingdom, leſſens the conſumption of corn, and thereby enables the nation to ſell a greater quantity of it to foreigners, and thus continually add to its riches by the commerce of ſo precious a production. It is, therefore, plain, that the eaſy circumſtances of the common people, in this manner, eſſentially contribute to the proſperity of the ſtate.

No diſtinction is made between the profits upon cattle and thoſe upon corn, in ſtating the income of the landlord, becauſe the rent of a farm is always regulated by what it can yield both in cattle and corn, in thoſe countries where the farmer's advances are not liable to be abſorbed by an arbitrary impoſt; for where the impoſt is payable by the farmer, the income ſuffers by it, the farmers dreading to make thoſe advances, which conſiſt in the purchaſe of cattle, for fear of bringing on themſelves a ruinous impoſition; the conſequence of which is, that tillage decays for want of a ſufficient quantity of cattle to make manures; and the expence of cultivating lands, impoveriſhed for want of proper manures, ſwallows up the produce,

duce, and leaves nothing for ſtate, church, or landlord.

THE profits upon cattle contribute ſo much to increaſe the yearly value of land, that one may be eſtimated by the other; and theſe two branches muſt not be ſeparated in computing the value of the produce in corn, by the income of the landlord; for the net produce, which yields both the rent, impoſt, and tithes, is to be obtained more eaſily by means of cattle, than by the labour of men, which alone could ſcarcely pay the charges of maintaining them. But great advances are neceſſary to purchaſe cattle; for which reaſon the government ſhould endeavour to invite riches rather than men, into the country. Men will never be wanting in fields, where riches are not wanting; whereas, take away riches, and you take away every thing; the lands loſe their value, and the kingdom its ſtrength and reſources.

THIS leads us to ſpeak of population, relatively to the order of the Table. But, as we are now ſpeaking of a country, where things are going to rack, I ſhall conſider po-

population in that cramped ſtate, to which the petty culture reduces it, and exhibit the totality of circulation upon that footing. Now, to make out the tranſition from that flouriſhing ſtate of cultivation and production, according to which we have hitherto directed our enquiries, to that wretched condition, into which we are going to fall, it is fit we ſhould previouſly make a ſhort calculation of the rapidity of the miſchiefs occaſioned by ſpoliation.

SECTION II.

The OECONOMICAL TABLE *considered relatively to a State of Spoliation.*

[See TABLE, N° IV.]

WE have been touching upon a kind of depredation, which has already done a great deal of mischief, and may do infinitely more, in proportion to the dominions and territory of a nation whose manners have a turn that way. After all, however important this article may be, it is not by its physical effects alone that it can so speedily ruin a nation, and reduce it to that degree of wretchedness, in which we are going to view it relatively to its produce. This it brings about much sooner by its moral effects, in as much as disorder infallibly introduces avidity, ever blind as to the means of attaining its ends. Spoliation is the real source of that decay of husbandry, whose effects are much more rapid and mischievous, than any calculation can make them appear.

By this word *ſpoliation* I underſtand every ſurcharge whatever, occaſioned by taxes or otherwiſe, that bears hard upon, and impairs, that ſtock, out of which the advances requiſite for tillage are to be ſupplied.

To adapt the Table to this hypotheſis, inſtead of ſuppoſing, that the king's, the church's, and the land-owner's ſhares of the net produce, are unequally divided between the productive and barren claſſes, we ſuppoſe that ſome of the blunders or misfortunes already mentioned, ſteals annually 2*l.* 10*s.* from the annual advances neceſſary for production. This defalcation reduces them to 50*l.* and it is on this footing that we have conſtructed the Table.

It appears by the recapitulation of the ſaid Table, that the total reproduce conſiſts of, 1ſt, 50*l.* for the king, the church, and the land-owner. 2dly, The annual advances amounting to as much more. 3dly, The intereſt of the annual and primitive advances, which, taken in the ſame progreſſion with the reſt, make 28*l.* 17*s.* Thus the total reproduction is but 128*l.* 17*s.*

By

BY comparing this produce with that given heretofore by the Table, when quite free from any burthen, it will appear, that whereas, in that happy condition, it yielded 135*l.* 5*s.* it will now, after the first year, yield but 128*l.* 17*s.* which is a decrease of 6*l.* 8*s.* in the reproduction. In fact there is a loss of 2*l.* 10*s.* on the net produce, 2*l.* 10*s.* on the annual advances, and 1*l.* 8*s.* on the interest of the annual and primitive advances, which makes in all a deficiency of 6*l.* 8*s.* and all this deficiency is occasioned by the primitive defalcation of 2*l.* 10*s.* only from the fund of annual advances. That the reader may not think himself at a gaming table, I must put him in mind, that our pounds stand for millions.

SUPPOSING that the scourge, by which we have so much suffered, is of a nature to hold for any length of time, we must continue our progression; and then it will appear, that, at the end of the second year, the spoliation, continued at the rate of 2*l.* 10*s.* will amount to 22*l.* 15*s.* at the end of the third to 64 *l.* 13 *s.* and at the end of the fourth to 171 *l.* 18 *s.*

THIS loſs, therefore, muſt ſoon affect the primitive advances, ſince the annual advances, amounting in the whole to but 52 *l.* 10 *s.* would in a ſhort time be entirely ſwallowed up; here then is a loſs of 265 *l.* 14 *s.* in four years, on the ſtock of primitive advances requiſite to ſet a plough agoing. We ſaid, that, in a good ſtate of culture, theſe advances might be rated at 500 *l.* therefore a plough, in four years, might be ſaid to be cut in two, that is, entirely diſabled, in the ſame manner that when one horſe in a heavy loaded coach and pair founders, the other muſt ſtand ſtill.

NOW, to avoid ſo great a misfortune, the huſbandman has recourſe to the wretched ſhift of ſtinting every branch of his advances, retrenching in point of manures, cattle, and ſervants; he plows with oxen or hobbies, and gives his land fewer and ſlighter dreſſings; but it is all one as to the produce; it is no matter in what part of the body a man receives

receives a wound, when the whole machine ſuffers by it. Thus in agriculture, let the fault lie where it will, whether in the farmer, in his operations, or in the quality of the ſeed he makes uſe of, a proportionable failure will appear in the crop, to the loſs of the huſbandman, the landlord, the church, and the ſovereign.

IF it ſhould be aſked, why a whole kingdom, in which agriculture declines in this manner, is not entirely waſte at the end of eight years? I anſwer, that the ſpoliation we are ſpeaking of, is a diſorder of arbitrary and ſucceſſive diſtribution, which does not ruin all the farmers at one ſtroke; it may be compared to a multitude of worms, which eat one by one the roots of the plants in a garden, and in time deſtroy it entirely. I might likewiſe anſwer it by the following compariſon. There never exiſted more cruel plunderers, at leaſt among thoſe who plunder openly, than the *Huns*; yet when the people of *Europe*, after repulſing theſe invaders, had the good fortune to force their ſtrong-holds in *Panonia*, they found them full of treaſure, which, though it bore no proportion to what had been deſtroyed by them all over *Europe*, was ſtill immenſe in proportion to the little that had eſcaped their fury. In like manner, every ſpoliation ſuppoſes ſome holes, where the ſpoils of the plundered are laid up. But, if theſe devaſtations happen to be ſo far authorized as to render the enjoying the fruits of them in the place where the harpies reſide, and if this place happens to be in the center of the plundered country, the conſumption and expences of every kind of the inhabitants of ſuch a place, cannot fail of keeping up life within its diſtrict, and ſupporting the great culture there for ſome time.

NAY the lands of ſuch diſtrict being employed in producing things of the firſt neceſſity, the delicacy and luxury of the inhabitants would make them ſeek out for things of the ſecond neceſſity at a greater diſtance. The ſun is not to be diſturbed in his operations, like earthly agents; he would ſtill produce oils in one province, exquiſite wines in another, and in a third give a reliſh extraordinary to partridges and ortolans; and the demand for theſe things would

carry

carry ſome ſmall ſparks of life to the otherwiſe ſtarved extremities.

THE ſame ſparks, whether iſſuing directly from the capital, or from other ſtore-houſes of baſtard ſubſiſtence, would ſtill enable ſome ſmall portions of land, ſurrounded with vaſt deſerts, to yield a net produce of 20 per cent. on the annual advances of cultivation; while in the diſtricts, employed in furniſhing a more immediate ſubſiſtence to the principal reſidence, there ſtill remained ſome parcels of land in the great culture.

ON the ſuppoſition, I ſay, of a legal and gradual ſpoliation, this principal reſidence would be ſtiled the capital. Now it appears, by the inductions already made, how mad it would be to think of reſtoring things reduced to this deſperate ſituation, by overloading the capital with taxes, from a notion, that by ſo doing the other parts of the kingdom would be eaſed, and ſupplied with hands, by the vaſt numbers, whom want of ſuſtenance would then oblige to forſake the capital. No, the wretches would ſooner lie down and ſtarve at the gates of it, than bury themſelves in deſerts. What can the indigent out-caſts of a city expect from agriculture, in countries where the inhabitants themſelves can find no employment? Nay, the new burthens laid upon the capital would ſerve only to wither its diſtrict, and dry up all the little branches of vivification, ſupplied by the expence of the inhabitants, and ſpreading to ſome diſtance.

WORSE and worſe ſtill would be the ſyſtem of the man, who, ſeeing the ſtate exhauſted, and without any reſource but a fictitious and ſtagnant kind of riches, ſhould attempt to diſcredit and annihilate ſuch corroſive riches, before he had found out any other to replace it with: not unlike an ignorant phyſician, who ſhould attempt to cure the pedicular diſeaſe, by killing the vermin as faſt as they iſſued from the patient's body, inſtead of endeavouring to reſtore the maſs of blood to its natural conſiſtence and circulation, which alone would ſoon put an end to the complaint. Thus, when a ſtate is poor and oppreſſed with debts, the government ſhould aſſiſt agriculture, break the numberleſs ſhackles with which the uſeful agents of that

that respectable class are loaded, honour the profession, have an eye to its success, and, above all things, engage men of sense and understanding to apply their thoughts and their riches that way, by exempting their advances from taxes, by affording a prospect of great profits to rich establishments, and every other possible method. But point out to those rich and now useless citizens, those petty retailers, those paper-blotters, brokers, and second rate financiers, with which our towns are now overstocked, and to the many others, who have taken refuge in them merely to save their little fortunes from an arbitrary and devouring impost, with which the inhabitants of the country are eaten up; but point out, I say, to these men, so greedy of the least profit, the vast treasures locked up in the bowels of the earth; protect them in their undertakings, their expences, and their endeavours, and they will fly in swarms to improve your lands. Besides, the land-owners themselves, especially the grandees of the kingdom, should lay themselves out to favour all attempts to cultivate that precious patrimony which is to secure to them the enjoyment of their rank and fortune, and free them from the neceſſity of looking out for other reſources leſs worthy of their great names, and withal leſs advantageous to the ſtate. By theſe methods, ſo certain and ſo well combined, you may again procure to your fields that opulence from which alone the land-owner, the ſtate, and the church, can expect a large income.

WE have been examining a very different conduct, in the rapid progreſs of the diſorders of ſpoliation, demonſtrated in the Table. Behold how a ſtate is reduced to the ſad impoſſibility of obtaining a greater produce than 20 per cent. on the advances of its agriculture; and that without any premeditated malice or evil deſigns in its governors, but merely from ſome capital miſtake in the firſt principles. Nay, ſuch a ſtate may think itſelf happy in the moderation of its governors, which, the minute the outcry becomes general, makes them often ſuſpend the moſt neceſſary operations, though, at the ſame time, no way diſproportionable to the opinion which they have a right to entertain

entertain of their primitive ſtrength. But for this moderation, the moſt fertile country would ſoon become as barren as the ſands of *Lybia*.

I AM now going to exhibit the conſequences of ſuch a degradation in agriculture, as, after yielding the huſbandman 10 per cent. on the primitive and annual advances, would leave but 20 per cent. on the annual advances for the ſtate, church, and land-owner.

SECTION

SECTION III.

The OECONOMICAL TABLE, *in which the Decay of Husbandry, and the sad Effects of such Declension, relatively to Population, are displayed.*

[See TABLE, N°. V.]

THIS is the chapter, which first convinced me that I was mistaken, and shewed me in what my mistake consisted. I had looked upon populousness as a source of incomes. An abler man contradicted me. It was my happiness to listen to him, and he has taught me, that, on the contrary, incomes were a source of populousness. If I have not altered my first work conformably to this notion, it is because by the mere weight of truth I recovered myself without assistance in the course of that very performance. It is likewise, because I thought it of little importance in the main to endeavour to conceal my error. It is, in fine, because

because I knew opportunities could not but offer of doing homage to truth; nor was it long before they did. I have already acquitted myself of this duty in a former discourse upon agriculture. I shall now reason upon, and calculate, the lie given to my own trophies.

I GREATLY doubt, if *Tullus Hostilius*, king of a country, in which, we are told, every family had an acre of land to supply it with cabbages and turnips, whenever they could not make war, and procure better subsistence, by plundering their neighbours; I doubt much, I say, if such a prince excelled in dignity an overseer of negroes, who, exclusive of their own wretched pittance, raise for their owner a very precious kind of commodity.

IT appears by the Table, that nothing can stir without the income; that it is the income, which constitutes the life and soul of the whole circulation. But no income is to be expected without great advances; and the advances themselves are not to be expected, unless the produce reaches the column of incomes.

IN

IN fact, the multiplicity and diversity of the different professions of mankind is not only an advantage relatively to the conveniencies of life, in procuring which each of these professions is separately employed, but likewise in as much as it confers the quality of riches upon products useless to one man, at the same time that they are useful to another in a different situation. Without ships we should have no occasion for ship-timber, nor without paint and soap for strong oils.

WE must recollect, that the usual propriety of things gives them the quality of goods, but that it is their venal value alone, which gives them that of riches. Water, wood, game, the fruits of the earth, &c. are goods; but the surplus of what the owner of them can consume, is no riches, unless a demand for such surplus gives it a venal value.

IT is this venal value which forms the relative state of riches between different kingdoms, and even different provinces of the same kingdom; between all the branches of foreign and domestic commerce. Without a relative proportion between the prices of different

ferent productions, there is no order of riches, that can counterballance the effects of a reciprocal commerce, decide the relative power of nations, and regulate both the produce of real estates, and the quantity of it due to the sovereign. For this reason, the venal value of the immediate fruits of the earth should be the principal object of every landed government's attention. Such governments are not to consider the usual value of these fruits, for their usual value never fails in rich nations; whereas, for want of a venal value, the advances, upon which the productions depend, fall to decay; the productions cease; indigence puts a stop to all the lucrative professions of people living in towns and cities; and reduces the inhabitants of the country to the ungrateful labours of a petty culture, whose pitiful produce is scarce sufficient for their own subsistence.

IT is the income that gives motion to every profession; it is, therefore, the income, that creates and excites the demands for every thing, and bestows the quality of riches on every kind of produce. It is

riches

riches that reftore the advances neceffary to procure a new product.

An author, who, in the beginning of this century, publifhed fome obfervations on the agriculture of a great kingdom, takes notice, that the advances did not produce, on an average, above twenty *per cent.* for the king, the church, and the land-owner, exclufive of the hufbandman's annual reimburfements, as ufual. Here, then, is a deficiency of four-fifths in the net produce, not to fpeak of the impoverifhment of the lands, obliged to bear themfelves all the expences of fuch wretched cultivation, and lie alternately fallow for feveral years together, to be again able to yield a pitiful crop. At this period, almoft all the inhabitants lived in a moft abject ftate of poverty, and were utterly loft to the ftate; *for the net produce of the labour of men, employed in agriculture, will be as the net produce of the advances above their expences; and the net produce for the king, church, and land-owner, and all the other claffes of men in a nation, will be as the net produce of the real eftates.* Thus, the more inſufficient the advances, the leſs profitable will both men and lands be to the ſtate. The moſt that can be expected from poor cottagers, who draw a wretched ſubſiſtence from an ungrateful cultivation, is to keep up in the country, to no purpoſe, a populouſneſs deſtitute of life and ſpirit.

IT is according to this ſtate of cultivation, that the Table now before us is conſtructed. We may ſee by it, how ſo ſlender a produce makes the whole circulation of a ſtate languiſh; and, as it is impoſſible for things to remain for ever in a languiſhing condition, it appears how near a nation, in ſuch a condition, muſt be to its end, relatively to its quality of a landed nation. Commerce, indeed, may ſupport it for ſome time, in appearance; but the maſter, who condeſcends to be a ſervant, may ſoon expect to ſee himſelf kicked out of the claſs of ſervants by thoſe, who are born to fill it.

IT is impoſſible for population not to deſcend through this ſcale of degradation; for, as man does not grow to the earth, and to dig and plow is his pennance, and not his

his employment, he is always looking out for ſome other to live by. Intereſt, however, will engage him to cultivate the earth, as long as he may do it by means of the animals created to ſerve him. But you, who would have a numerous people, offer them other employments, and take care to procure yourſelf, by judicious and ſtout cultivation, an income ſufficient to reward their induſtry.

THE ruling idea of war makes nations fancy, that ſtrength conſiſts entirely in populouſneſs; but the military part of a nation cannot act, or even ſubſiſt, without the aſſiſtance of the labouring part. As little is it to be ſuppoſed, that the riches of a ſtate depends on the number of its ſubjects. No, it is only by means of riches that men can acquire and perpetuate riches, and that only as far, as there is a juſt proportion between men and riches.

NATIONS are too apt never to think themſelves populous enough; they never ſo much as dream, that they want work or wages to ſupport a greater population; and that men of no fortune are uſeleſs in a country, where they cannot find ſuch certain wages as may enable them to live by their labour.

It is true, indeed, that the common people in the country, when not employed by others, may make a ſhift to raiſe for their ſubſiſtence ſome few things of little value, which require neither great expences, nor a labour of any continuance; and, beſides, take up but little time to arrive at maturity; but theſe men, theſe productions, and the lands yielding them, are of no account in regard to the ſtate.

For the earth to yield any income, it is requiſite, that the labour of the huſbandman ſhould give a net produce, after paying him for his trouble; for it is this net produce that ſupports the other claſſes of men neceſſary in a ſtate. Now there is no expecting this from poor peaſants, who till the earth with their hands, or in any other inſufficient manner. They have enough to do to procure a pitiful ſubſiſtence for themſelves alone,

alone, without ever attempting wheat, which requires too much time, too much labour, and too great an expence, to be raiſed by men, who have nothing but the labour of their hands to raiſe it with. It is not, therefore, to a ſet of wretched peaſants, that you ſhould leave the cultivation of your lands. Beaſts alone ſhould till and fertilize your fields. Nothing but a plentiful conſumption, a ready vent, and a free and eaſy commerce, both foreign and domeſtic, can ſecure that venal value which conſtitutes your income.

IT is upon rich men alone that you ought to depend for the eſtabliſhing of a cultivation, and rural commerce, capable of enriching you, of enriching the ſtate, and of opening a never-failing ſource of riches, by means of which you may ſecure to yourſelf a full enjoyment of all the fruits of both huſbandry and handicraft labour, fortify your frontiers, and have always ſtrong armies, and formidable fleets, at your diſpoſal; carry on, in a grand manner, the public works neceſſary for uſe and ornament, and afford ſuch wages and profits, as may tempt induſtrious foreigners to ſettle in the kingdom.

THUS, on the police of agriculture, and the commerce of its productions, depends the management of the finances, and of all the other branches of adminiſtration, in a landed ſtate.

NUMEROUS armies are not alone ſufficient to form a ſtrong defence. Without good pay, you are not to expect good ſoldiers.

A WAR by ſea or by land employs other means, beſides the ſtrength of men, and requires other, and more conſiderable expences, beſides that of ſubſiſting them; ſo that war is to be ſupported much leſs by the dint of men, than that of riches; for as long as you have riches to pay men well, you will never want men to recruit your armies.

THE more riches a nation can employ in the annual reproduction of riches, the fewer men, in proportion, will ſuch annual repro-

duction

duction require; and the greater the net produce of agriculture, the more men will be at the disposal of the government for public works, and every other public service; the higher wages are, the more useful will these men be to the state by their labour, and by their expences, which carry these wages back into circulation.

VICTORIES, in which you do your enemy no other mischief, but kill him men, can weaken him but little, as long as he has wherewith to invite others into his service. An army of 100,000 men may be as good as an army of a million; for no army, where pay never fails, can ever be destroyed. It then, too, becomes the interest of the soldiers to stick to their colours, since they cannot expect better pay in any other service. It is, therefore, riches that supports the honour of arms, and recruits armies; and with how much more reason must riches be allowed to support and extend every other kind of population?

LET us again give a look at the Table, in order to be convinced of the sad condition, to which an unprofitable cultivation reduces both the proprietary and handicraft claſs, and judge what muſt be the ſtate of populouſneſs, when the whole territory has no other ſubſiſtence to offer its inhabitants, but the few wretched and precarious neceſſaries, ſuited to the meaneſt claſs of labourers, required by a cultivation incapable of yielding any net produce.

LET us now examine, if money, which is ſo much idolized, can, on this occaſion, ſupply the place of real riches.

SECTION IV.

The OECONOMICAL TABLE *considered in its Disorders relative to Money.*

[See TABLE, No. V.]

—— *Parvis componere magna solebam.*

WE are wont to calculate the riches of states, as we do that of individuals; and, because a private man, who has money, has all, or almost all, manner of physical goods at his command, we imagine it must be the same in regard to nations. But suppose this private man, transported with all his gold and silver, into the heart of some desert. He would there infallibly perish with cold and hunger, tho' seated upon this treasure, which he had purchased with other riches: (for money is bought, and no man can have it, but in proportion as he has other riches to pay for it) therefore, to acquire money, is not to acquire riches; it is only changing one kind of riches for another; which shews, that

that it is the neighbourhood of other goods, and the conveniency of exchanging money for them, that gives to money the quality of riches.

THOUGH the rich man, above mentioned, had millions at his disposal, if, when pressed by necessity, two persons were to present themselves before him, one with bread, and the other with water, and refused him the least quantity of either, for less than his whole treasure, he would be obliged to come into their terms, and part with all for a day's subsistence.

NOW, this individual is a true picture of the state which has lost its produce; with this difference, that the individual retains his gold and silver, whereas a nation, which has no stock of riches left, cannot be supposed to have either, unless it can draw them directly from the earth.

MONEY, that species of riches which is purchased with other riches, is nothing in a nation, *but an intermediate pledge between buyers and sellers*, which ceases to contribute

to

to the perpetuation of riches in a ſtate, the moment it ceaſes to circulate, or yield riches for riches. Nay, in this caſe, the more it is hoarded up, the more riches it coſt, by putting a ſtop to the renewal of riches, and, conſequently, the more it impoveriſhes a nation.

MONEY, therefore, is no better than an active kind of riches, which is of no real advantage to a ſtate, but in proportion as it continually yields riches for riches. The ſole uſe of it in a ſtate, is to facilitate ſales and purchaſes, and the payment of the king's, the church's, and the land-owner's income, which again make it circulate; ſo that the ſame money ſerves continually, and in rotation, for theſe payments, and the purpoſes of commerce.

THUS the maſs of money, in a landed ſtate, is ever found to be nearly equal to the net produce, or annual income of its lands; for even in this proportion it is more than ſufficient to anſwer all the purpoſes of the nation. A greater quantity of money would be be no riches to the ſtate. For tho' the impoſt is paid in money, it is not money that yields it, but the riches which the lands are annually reproducing. It is in the amount of theſe perpetually renaſcent riches, and not in the amount of its money, as the vulgar think, that the proſperity and ſtrength of a nation conſiſt.

MONEY cannot indemnify a ſtate for any deficiency in the ſucceſſive renovation of this kind of riches; whereas the place of money is eaſily ſupplied, in trade, by engagements in writing, ſecured by the riches poſſeſſed in the country, and exportable to foreign markets.

THE love of money is a very ſtrong paſſion in individuals, who forget they were obliged to buy it, becauſe they are indiſcreetly greedy of that which purchaſes other riches. But this kind of greedineſs, excluſive of its object, ought not to be the paſſion of the ſtate.

A GREAT ſtock of money is no further deſirable in a ſtate, than as it is proportioned to the income, and thereby indicates perpetual reproduction

reproduction of opulence, the employment of which is real, and perfectly ſecure. Of this kind was that plenty of money, which, in the reign of our *Charles* V. ſirnamed *The Wiſe*, kept pace with the plenty of every other kind of riches in the kingdom. We may form ſome idea of it, by the riches ſpecified in the immenſe inventory of that prince, excluſive of a reſerve of 1,350,000 *l.* (equal to about 12,500,000*l.* of our money at preſent) which was found in his coffers; theſe great riches are ſo much the more remarkable, as one third of the kingdom of *France*, ſuch as it then was, did not bring him in any thing.

MONEY, therefore, is not to be conſidered as the riches of a ſtate, as that riches which is continually conſuming and ſpringing up again; for money does not engender money. A crown well employed may, it is true, give birth to riches worth two crowns; but then it is the riches acquired by means of the money, and not the money itſelf, that has multiplied. It is only by yielding riches for riches, that money may be ſaid to give birth to new riches. Money, therefore, ought not to ſtagnate in idle hands.

IT is not, therefore, ſuch matter of indifference to the ſtate, into what hands money gets; for it is abſolutely neceſſary, that it ſhould not be wreſted from him, who employs it for the benefit of the ſtate. But, ſtrictly ſpeaking, money thus employed in a nation, has no owner; it is to anſwer the demands of the ſtate, which make it circulate for the reproduction of riches capable of yielding ſubſiſtence to the nation, and tribute to the ſovereign.

WE are not to confound this money with that devouring wealth, whoſe owners do nothing with it but lend it out at intereſt, thus eluding that contribution, which every real income owes to the ſtate.

THE money, of neceſſity, has, I ſay, with every individual, a deſtination to which it deciſively belongs. That, which is deſtined to the actual payment of the impoſt, belongs to the impoſt; that, which is deſtined to make any neceſſary purchaſe, belongs to that purchaſe; that, which gives life to agriculture, commerce, and induſtry, belongs to agriculture, commerce, and induſtry; that, which is to pay a debt, which is already, or or will soon be due, belongs to that debt, &c. and not to the person who has it. It is the nation's money. No individual has a right to lend it, because it does not belong to any individual.

IT is, nevertheless, this money scattered here and there, which forms the principal mass of wealth of a truly opulent kingdom, in which it is constantly employed for the advantage of the state. Nay, people do not scruple to sell it for more than it has cost them; that is to say, to export it to purchase foreign commodities, when they yield a sure profit; nor are foreigners unacquainted with the advantages of this trade, in which profit decides whether money shall be given for commodities, or commodities for money; for in all places money and commodities are riches, merely in proportion to their venal value.

MONEY, that lies idle, that cannot be reproduced, is an inconsiderable object, soon exhausted by a small multiplication of loans. It is money, nevertheless, that is perpetually dazzling the vulgar; it is this object alone, that they consider as the riches of a nation, and as a great resource in the exigencies of

a state,

a ſtate, even a great ſtate, which cannot be really rich, but by the net reproduce of thoſe riches, which its lands annually afford. It is this produce, which, as it were, gives new birth to money, by renewing it, and conſtantly accelerating its circulation.

BESIDES, every kingdom, which the export of its productions has enriched, has, by means of the correſpondence it keeps up with other kingdoms, a ſtock of riches in them, and may every where make money out of paper.

THE plenty and free ſale of its productions ſecure to it, therefore, the uſe of the money belonging to other countries; and, in a well cultivated kingdom, money is never wanting to pay the king, church, and land-owner their ſhare in the net produce of thoſe commodities fit for trade, which the earth is conſtantly reproducing. But tho' money is never wanting to pay them, we muſt not miſtake the matter, and imagine, that the tribute due to the king may be impoſed upon money.

A GOVERNMENT, therefore, ſhould never confine its views to money. It ought to look

look further, and beſtow its chief attention on the plenty and venal value of the productions of the earth, in order to encreaſe as much as poſſible its net produce. It is in this portion of viſible and annual riches, that the power and opulence of the monarch, and the proſperity of the nation, conſiſt; it is what fixes the ſubjects, and ties them down to their native ſoil.

MONEY, the labour of the handicraftsman, trade, and commerce, form but a baſtard and independent domain, which, without the riches of the ſoil, can only conſtitute a republican ſtate. *Conſtantinople* itſelf, though no republican government, by being reduced to the moveable riches of traffic, has, in the midſt of deſpotiſm, the genius and independence of a republic, in regard to the looſe and unſtable ſtate of correſpondences, and commercial riches.

LET us, therefore, ſtrip money of all the properties attributed to it by prejudice; for they are altogether imaginary. We may as well attribute to a whip the power of drawing a coach, becauſe it puts in motion the ſix horſes that really draw it; place the whip between ſix trees, and ſee if it will make them ſtir. In the ſame manner, money works miracles in places, where there is a briſk barter of neceſſaries. For example, a man at Paris, who to-day has nothing but gold, may to-morrow, if he pleaſes, have plate, ſervants, and a ſumptuous table; but place him in ſome of the provinces, and it will take him a month to prepare for an elegant entertainment.

MONEY, therefore, is riches merely in virtue of its permutability: nor can it have this value but in proportion to the demand for it, which demand will always be as the quantity of barter; therefore the quantity of money in a country will be as the circulation of riches and neceſſaries: at leaſt, one may ſay of money that does not circulate, what is ſaid in the fable of the miſer's hidden treaſure; *Put a ſtone in its place, and it will be worth you as much.*

THIS granted, let us return to our Table, and ſurvey it in the wretched condition to which

which it has been reduced by a paltry cultivation, that yields but one-fifth of the annual advances, besides the said annual advances, and 10 per cent. on them and the primitive advances; and let us examine how far the circulation now extends, and how much it is impaired; for then we may judge what quantity of money, in such a country, is really employed in the service of the public.

No doubt, a nation reduced to so low an ebb, in regard to its stock, may still afford a retreat in some parts of its territories to those communities of merchants, whose industry borrows motion from foreign countries, and still imparts some action to the neighbouring districts; and some of those merchants may possibly accumulate pecuniary fortunes to the prejudice of the annual reproduction of riches. The depredations committed, in levying the public revenue, may likewise produce some stores of money, *the melancholy remains of the best blood* of the nation; fortunes, which, however shocking to those who only consider how ill they become their owners, are nothing in the main to the riches by them abſorbed in a great ſtate. They are indeed money; but then it is ſo much money diverted from the purpoſes of reproduction, and which never would have been accumulated, had it found a place in circulation, which can only receive of it in proportion to the quantity of circulating and renaſcent riches; ſuch riches, in a word, as are to be repreſented, conſumed, and reproduced: it cannot, I ſay, re-enter this circulation, weakened at its ſource, till all the money actually circulating ſhall have been pumped out of it, till it fails, in fine, and extreme neceſſity obliges people to replace it by purchaſing it back at a rate, that makes the remedy worſe than the diſeaſe.

THIS misfortune muſt quickly happen in a nation, which has loſt its renaſcent riches, ſo as to find itſelf much in the ſame condition with the man we juſt now ſuppoſed in a deſart, with nothing but money to eat and drink. On ſuch occaſions recourſe muſt be had to the money lying dead in private hands; but the ſtate can only borrow it

from

from week to week, and muſt, beſides, give good ſecurity for the loan of it. This is every day the caſe. But the huſbandman muſt not borrow; for borrowing would ruin him, or, at leaſt, the intereſt of what he borrowed ſhould be deducted from the net produce to the prejudice of the proprietary claſs, as otherwiſe it would eat up the huſbandman's annual re-imburſements and reſources. Thus the farmer can truſt to nothing but his own riches for a ſolid and certain eſtabliſhment. Hence the ruin of the farmer is always attended with the ruin of agriculture, the ruin of the landlord, and the ruin of the ſtate, how opulent ſoever the financier, the uſurer, and the ſtock-broker may be; and, after all, this opulence of theirs is no better than the poor remains of the immenſe riches, raviſhed by theſe harpies from the important purpoſes of reproduction.

SUCH is the point of view in which money is to be conſidered in a ſtate; and ſuch is all its influence, every way incapable of regenerating a nation, which obſtructs, or even neglects, the great buſineſs of reproduction.

SECTION

SECTION V.

The OECONOMICAL TABLE *considered in its Disorders relatively to the Police.*

[See TABLE, N° V.]

WE still leave before our readers the Table in that state of declension, to which a poor and insufficient cultivation has brought it, as we are going to enquire into the causes of that wretchedness to which such a decay of agriculture is owing; a decay, that is constantly accelerating in proportion to its continuance.

THE man, who has by this ever so little acquired a facility of arguing in the manner adopted by us in the Table, must easily discern, that moral as well as physical causes may serve to overturn the balance in the article of expences, and by increasing the share of the barren class, proportionably dry up the sources of the proprietary class, upon whose wealth that of the barren class itself, in the end, totally depend.

IT

IT is obvious, for example, that law-expences ought to be placed in the class of barren expences, and that whatever tends to increase expences of that kind must, for that very reason, be a cause of decay. Hence it follows, that in a country where the laws are so faulty, that every head landlord, or under landlord, is obliged to be in continual motion, to obtain justice or injustice, favour or advancement, &c. the expences created thereby are so many weights taken from the scale of productive expences, and thrown into the scale of barren expences, which must of course preponderate. If, moreover, dissoluteness and effeminacy happen to prevail to such a degree, as to extinguish all respect for domestic hierarchy, and render unthinking youth the arbiter of family expences, it is probable that these expences will be double what they ought to be in the barren purchase of trifles and luxuries; whereas provident age delights in what is solid and useful. And this evil, once become general, cannot, on account of the great number of co-operating causes, but be attended with a very considerable decay.

WERE

WERE the laws to favour this evil by the connivance, however, involuntary, of those charged with the interpretation of them; were the police, under the pretext of foreseeing every thing, to free the child from all parental, and the servant from all magisterial restraints; were it to provoke taste for barren expences, under the notion of increasing the profits of the retailers and artificers of luxury; were it to abandon the honest peasant to contempt, oppression, and poverty, and thereby ruin husbandry; were it to favour the multiplication of law-suits, and multiply the terrible tools of chicane, in order to increase the stamp duties; were it to lower the price of the immediate fruits of the earth to support manufactures; were it to annihilate the sale, venal value, and reproduction of commodities, by heavy imposts upon them, &c. all these things might be justly considered as so many disorders in manners, omens of ruin, and excressences of barren expences.

IT is thus, that by a single glance of the understanding upon our Table, a man may, in an instant, discover the real value of every

every law, of every civil ordinance, even thoſe which do not appear to have any other than a moral tendency. But the conciſeneſs of this explanation will not permit us to enlarge further on this head; let us, therefore, return to the phyſical points of police, more immediately connected with the object of our preſent enquiry.

THERE is no abſurdity, which a ſpirit of refinement, grafted upon wrong principles, is not capable of engendering. I would not take upon me to ſwear, that with a little pains we might not diſcover ſome landed ſtates, in which private views had ſo far led people aſtray, as to make them believe, it was proper to reſtrain the cultivation of vines to increaſe that of wheat; and that, too, at a time, when the exportation of corn was forbid, and even the domeſtic commerce of it between province and province obſtructed; at a time, when moſt of the lands lay fallow, becauſe the cultivation of corn was confined to the conſumption of the province that produced it; at a time, in ſhort, when the decay of vine-culture, and the impoſt

impoſt upon wine, increaſed the fallow lands from one year to another.

IT is very poſſible, that in theſe circumſtances the provinces remote from the capital ſhould have been obliged to make repreſentations againſt the increaſe of tillage, as their corn, for want of ſale, became a drug upon their hands, to the utter ruin of both farmers and land-owners, and the annihilation of the impoſt the lands were charged with. Thus every thing conſpired to wither the two principal branches of cultivation of the kingdom, and ſink to nothing the value of real eſtates; ſome of the land-owners endeavouring to procure excluſive privileges of culture, to the prejudice of the reſt; fatal effects of prohibitions and obſtructions, affecting the commerce of the productions of landed eſtates, eſpecially in a kingdom, where there is ſuch an eaſy communication between the provinces by ſea and by rivers, where the capital, and all the other cities, can be ſo eaſily ſupplied with proviſions from every part of its territories, and where the facility of exportation ſecures a ready ſale for all its ſuperfluities.

THERE

THERE is no branch of country business equal to the cultivation of vines; for, in general, the net produce of an acre under vines is, at least, double that of the best acre under corn. We are, besides, to take notice, that the charges required by the former are of a more beneficial nature, than those required by the latter; because the culture of vines affords, even with profit to the employer, much better wages to the hands employed in it, because the demand for poles and casks creates a demand for timber; and, lastly, because the hands employed in the cultivation of vines are not taken up by it in harvest time, and are, therefore, a great resource to the husbandman, in getting in his corn.

BESIDES, this class of men, being paid for their labour in the produce of the land itself, and by growing very numerous, increase the demand for both corn and wine, and keeps up the venal value of these articles, in proportion as the cultivation extends, and such increase of cultivation increases riches; for the increase of riches is attended with an increase of populousness in every rank of of the ſtate, and this increaſe of populouſneſs ſupports, on all hands, the venal value of the immediate productions of the earth, and, conſequently, the income of the king, the church, and the land-owners.

IT is to be noted, that a facility of exporting the immediate productions of the earth, free from heavy taxes and duties, is a great advantage to a nation bleſſed with an extenſive territory, in which the culture may be ſo varied, as to make it yield a great variety of valuable commodities, ſuch, eſpecially, as cannot grow in the neighbouring countries.

UNRIVALLED, therefore, as we are in the production of wines and brandies, through the nature of our ſoil and climate, the exportation of them ſhould be particularly favoured by the government, inſtead of being loaded, as it is, with heavy burthens, multiplied to the great loſs of the revenue itſelf, and too prejudicial to the vent of productions, which form the object of a great foreign trade, a trade capable of ſupporting the opulence of a great kingdom. The impoſt ſhould be ſimple and unincumbered,

and

and laid on the ſoil, which produces theſe riches; and in the repartition of the general impoſt, regard ſhould be had to thoſe commodities, whoſe ſale in foreign markets depends upon the reaſonableneſs of their price; for then the ſtate is amply indemnified for the ſmallneſs of ſuch impoſt, by the advantageous influence of this commerce upon all the kingdom's other ſources of riches. But let us not anticipate the article of impoſts.

I SHOULD be wanting to myſelf, as a man, if, ſpeaking of the police in general, I omitted ſaying a word or two of that terrible ſcourge, one of the three which God was pleaſed to give the choice of to ſinful *David*, and to which this prince preferred the plague; I mean the *police of corn*. I ſee only with the eyes of a calculator.

BY putting a ſtop to the exportation of corn, and other immediate productions of the earth, you confine your agriculture to your ſtate of populouſneſs, inſtead of making your agriculture a means of increaſing your populouſneſs.

THE

THE exportation of the immediate fruits of the earth increases the annual value of real estates; this increase of their annual value increases the expence of the land-owners; this increase of expence draws people into the kingdom; this increase of populousness, increases the consumption of the immediate fruits of the earth; this increase of consumption, along with exportation, accelerates on all sides the progress of agriculture, populousness, and increases, in its turn, the annual value of real estates.

BY means of a free and easy exportation and importation, corn is always kept at an equal price; for the most equal price is that, which prevails most universally among trading nations. Such a commerce ever compensates the casual inequalities in the crops of different nations, by bringing to that country, where any scarcity happens, the superfluity of that where plenty prevails; thus making the quantity of productions, and the prices of them, always and every where equal.

HENCE,

Hence, trading nations, that have no lands to ſupply them with corn, are, notwithſtanding, as ſecure of bread, as thoſe which cultivate a large territory. Freedom of commerce, and the leaſt advantage in point of price, muſt infallibly draw goods into a country, and by that means keep things conſtantly at, or very near, the ſame ſtandard.

Now, it has been demonſtrated, that, independently of exportation, and even the advantage of a better price, a conſtant equality of price is alone ſufficient to increaſe, by one-ſixth, the net produce of real eſtates; that it increaſes and ſecures the advances of cultivation; that it prevents exceſſive dearths, which hurt populouſneſs, and that it hinders commodities from becoming a drug, to the prejudice of agriculture; whereas, a prohibition of foreign trade is often attended with a dearth of neceſſaries; a cultivation too nicely adjuſted to the annual demands of a nation, reduces the price of proviſions to the ſame fluctuation, that is occaſioned in the harveſt by good or bad weather, and brings great part of the lands to yield little, and be be worth little; the uncertainty of ſale creates uneaſineſs among the farmers, puts a ſtop to the expences of cultivation, lowers the rent of land; and this decay increaſes from day to day, in the ſame proportion with the inſidious precautions, taken to prevent it.

IF, by way of preventing a ſcarcity of corn, the government ſhould not only forbid the exportation of it, but hinder dealers from filling their granaries with it in plentiful ſeaſons, which ought to provide againſt bad ones, and likewiſe obſtruct the multiplication of thoſe free magazines, where the competition of dealers renders a monopoly impoſſible; procures the huſbandman a market in times of plenty, and produces plenty in the midſt of ſterility: then, from the ſelf-ſame principles of ſuch a timorous adminiſtration, and ſo ill adapted to a landed nation, which nothing but a ready ſale of, and a good price for its productions, can enrich; from the ſelf-ſame principles, I ſay, we may as fairly conclude, that it would be equally proper to reſtrain, as much as poſſible, the home-conſumption of corn, by reducing the common people to the uſe of potatoes, black wheat, acorns, and the like; and even make it a crime to ſend corn from the provinces where it abounded, into thoſe which wanted it, and which had been robbed of it, by ſpecial or furtive licences.

WHAT abuſes, what monopolies, muſt flow from ſuch an arbitrary, and deſtructive police! What would then become of agriculture, of the proprietary and manufacturing claſſes of men, of the ſtrength of the kingdom?

I SHALL not repeat in this place, what has been ſaid ſo often, in anſwer to the miſtaken apprehenſions of ſome people concerning the danger of corn's becoming too dear for the common people. If the ſummary demonſtrations, which reſult from the explanation of the Table, are not found ſufficient to remove them, the reader may conſult what I have written more at large upon this ſubject, in the diſcourſe I had the honour of preſenting to the ſociety at *Berne*.

THIS naturally leads us to the article of commerce.

SECTION VI.

The OECONOMICAL TABLE *considered in its Depredations relatively to Commerce.*

[See TABLE, N°. V.]

COMMERCE so far resembles light, that, though it creates nothing, it gives life to all things.

WE should here recollect, what has been already said concerning the difference between *goods* and *riches*. A distinction ought to be made in every state between *goods* which have an *usual* value, but no *venal* value, and riches which have both an *usual* and a *venal* value. For example, the savages of *Louisiana* had great plenty of goods; such as water, wood, game, the fruits of the earth, *&c.* these, however, could not be called riches, as they had no venal value: but since some branches of trade have been opened betwen them and the *French*, the

 English,

English, and the *Spaniards*, &c. part of theſe goods have acquired a venal value, and of courſe the quality of riches.

THUS *the government of every kingdom ought to aim at procuring to its ſubjects the greateſt plenty poſſible of productions, and to theſe productions the greateſt venal value poſſible*; becauſe with great riches a nation, by means of commerce, may procure all manner of uſual goods, beſides gold and ſilver, in a proportion ſuitable to its riches.

WE are not to conſider commerce as an increaſe of ſtock. It is true, indeed, that a reciprocal commerce with foreigners brings in commodities, but theſe commodities muſt one way or another be paid for by the nation. Commerce, therefore, is not to be conſidered as a ſeparate object in the detail of a kingdom's income. It is with commerce as with houſe-rent, and intereſt of money, which are, to thoſe who pay them, expences that ariſe from another ſource. It is otherwiſe, indeed, with regard to land-charges, which are laid upon a productive fund; but then theſe land-charges are included

cluded in the net produce of the lands. The earth, and the farmer's advances for the cultivation of it, are the only ſource of incomes in a landed nation; but theſe incomes would vaniſh into ſmoke, were it not for the value which commerce gives to the fruits of the earth; nay, in a ſhort time, theſe fruits would be confined to the ſlender conſumption of the maſter.

DOMESTIC commerce, is, properly ſpeaking, what we ſtile circulation; and that circulation is moſt beneficial which conſiſts in buying and ſelling at the firſt hand; for the oftener the ſame thing is bought and ſold, though the buyers and ſellers ſhould be ſubjects of the ſame ſtate, the more does domeſtic commerce become onerous to them. And it is in this light we ought to conſider the merit of a tradeſman in the domeſtic commerce of a nation.

THE foreign trade, or that of exportation, may extend, as appears by the explanation of the Table, to about one-eighth of the total annual produce of the earth. This exportation may be termed actual, if ſuch eighth part is exported in kind; and virtual, if it is conſumed at home by handicrafts-men, whoſe works are exported. Such is the general idea of the commerce of a landed ſtate, conſidered in its riſe, in its growth, and in its uſefulneſs.

Commerce, therefore, gives life and the quality of riches to the immediate productions of the earth, and of courſe exiſtence to the incomes and power of a nation. But we are not to confound in the idea, which we form to ourſelves of this great political agent, all thoſe ſubſervient agents, which a landed nation can very well diſpenſe with. By this means we ſhould little by little deify the inſects bread in the mud of this *Nile*, ſuch as ſtocks, agio, &c.

Not to ſpeak of theſe laſt, which are no better than ſo many evolutions of uſury, the others, which are uſeful to nations that have no territory, and even to landed ſtates, which have more ſubjects than the plough and ſpade can employ, don't deſerve the direct attention of the government. The head of of a great landed ſtate, who ſhould employ his power to render his ſubjects a trading people, to the excluſion of all others, might be compared to a man of fortune, who ſhould take it into his head to drive his own coach, and cook his own victuals, to ſave the wages of a coachman and a cook.

How many wars might have been avoided in the laſt century, and might ſtill perhaps be avoided, would people but conſider the petty commercial ſtates as the commercial agents of the great ones, and be perſuaded that it is more advantageous for the firſt to trade by means of the ſecond, than to charge themſelves with the different branches of commerce, which cannot fail of proving more expenſive, and leſs profitable to them, than it would be to procure themſelves, at their own doors, a great competitorſhip of foreign merchants, and thereby effectually prevent all monopolies by their own merchants.

ADURAM, comptroller-general of the finances of the late king *Solomon*, unfortunately

nately dazzled by the commerce of the *Tyrians*, and the ſplendor of luxurious manufactures, raiſed ſuch a ferment in the brains of all his countrymen, that they no longer ſpoke of any thing but commerce and money, without ever ſo much as dreaming of the true and genuine commerce of their country.

THIS miniſter, valuable in other reſpects for his good intentions, but too attached to his own way of thinking, ſet about ſqueezing riches from the work of the fingers, even to the prejudice of the true ſource of riches, and for this purpoſe diſturbed the whole œconomical conſtitution of a landed nation. The exportation of corn was prohibited, to enable the manufacturer to live cheap. The corn-trade at home was put into the hands of an arbitrary police, which interrupted the commerce between the provinces. The protectors of handicraft buſineſs, the intendant of provinces, and the magiſtrates of cities, in order to procure themſelves corn at an eaſy rate, ruined, in conſequence of a miſtaken calculation, both their towns and their provinces,

vinces, by insensibly lessening the culture of their lands. Every measure tended to the destruction of land-rents, handicraft-works, manufactures; and even commerce, which, in a landed state, can only be supported by the produce of the land; for it is this produce which supplies commerce with superfluities for exportation, and which pays the landlord his rent, the sovereign his tribute, the church her tithes, and the salaries of those employed in lucrative works. Various emigrations of men and riches accelerated the progress of this destruction. Both men and money were diverted from agriculture, and applied to manufactures of cotton, silk, and foreign wools, to the prejudice of the manufactures carried on with the wools of the country, and the multiplication of cattle. Great pains were taken to provoke the luxury of decoration, and it accordingly made very hasty strides. The administrators of the provinces, pressed by the exigencies of the state, no longer permitted the countryman to enjoy any security in the visible employment of the riches necessary to the annual reproduction of riches. A great part of the lands were permitted to fall into

petty

petty culture, to lie fallow, to ſink to nothing; land-rents were ſacrificed to no manner of purpoſe to a mercantile commerce, incapable of contributing to the impoſt. And as huſbandry, impaired and oppreſſed, could no longer give the ſtate any aſſiſtance, the burthens of it were more and more laid upon men, upon proviſions, and upon the commerce carried on in the immediate fruits of the earth; the expences and piracies attending the perception of ſuch taxes, daily encreaſed, and at length became the object of a ſyſtem of finances, which enriched the capital with the ſpoils of the provinces. Money-lending became a trade from which people drew yearly incomes, founded on money, and drawn from money, which, with reſpect to the nation, conſtituted no better than an imaginary produce, that eſcaped the impoſt, and preyed upon the ſtate. Theſe incomes accruing from money, and a ſhew of opulence, ſupported by the magnificence of a ruinous luxury, impoſed upon the vulgar, while, from day to day, they, in fact, leſſened the reproduction of real riches, and the money of the nation.

EVERY

EVERY body knows what happened ſoon after *Solomon's* death. Had he lived longer, he would have died a bankrupt, and the *Holy-Land*, formerly ſo fruitful, would have been long ſince over-run with briars and brambles.

MANUFACTURES for home conſumption are no better than an object of expence, and by no means a ſource of income; nor can the exportation of them afford any net profit, but to countries where manual labour is cheap, in conſequence of the cheapneſs of proviſions neceſſary for the ſubſiſtence of manufacturers; a very diſadvantageous condition for the produce of real eſtates: and accordingly ſuch cheapneſs is to be carefully avoided in ſtates which enjoy a free and foreign commerce, by which the demand for, and price of, the immediate fruits of the earth, is kept up; a circumſtance, which deſtroys to advantage the trifling net produce deriveable from the exportation of manufactures, as the profits of ſuch an exportation can only reſult from the under value of the immediate fruits of the earth.

WE don't confound in this place the general net produce or income belonging to the nation, with the profits of merchants, and master-manufacturers. These profits are to be considered as barren expences, with respect to the nation. For example, what would it signify to have rich husbandmen, if the lands cultivated by them yielded for none but themselves.

THERE are some poor nations, in which most of the manufactures of luxury, multiplied to too great a degree, are supported by exclusive privileges, by laying the nation under contribution, by means of prohibitions, which deprive them of the use of other handicraft commodities. It is not so with agriculture, and the commerce carried on in the immediate fruits of the earth, where the briskest competitorship multiplies the riches of nations blest with extensive territories.

PRINCES should encourage those manufactures alone, whose materials are found in the country, and can therefore be made up cheaper there than elsewhere; and they should

ſhould permit the purchaſe from foreigners of ſuch manufactures, as foreigners can afford for leſs than their ſubjects can make them up. By this means they would provoke a reciprocal commerce; whereas, by pretending to ſell every thing, and buy nothing, they would ſoon put an end to all foreign commerce, and deprive their ſubjects of the advantage of exporting the immediate fruits of their lands; an advantage infinitely preferable to that of exporting manufactures.

A LANDED nation ſhould favour the exportation of the immediate fruits of the earth, by the importation of manufactures which ſhe can turn to advantage from foreigners. Herein lies the whole myſtery of commerce. Let us but act in this manner, and we need not be under any apprehenſions of *becoming tributary to other nations.*

BUT enough of commerce. It appears, by the ill ſucceſs of *Aduram*'s ſchemes, how dear the moſt knowing, moſt upright, and moſt diligent miniſters may, by miſtaking the firſt principles, pay for a tranſient eclat, and momentary enjoyment, ſo as to ſap the

foundations

foundations of a powerful ſtate. *Azmoth*, on the contrary, miniſter of the warlike *David*, who had conquered his kingdom foot by foot, by applying himſelf to the encouragement of agriculture, and living upon good terms with the *Tyrians*, though he had neither a fleet at *Aſion Gaber*, nor any manufactures at *Jericho*; *Azmoth*, I ſay, had in a ſhort time the happineſs to ſee his fellow-ſubjects a flouriſhing people, and left behind him a great treaſure to build the temple.

BUT as we have mentioned king *David*, let us now touch the main ſtring of the œconomical harp.

SECTION VII.

The OECONOMICAL TABLE *considered in its Depredations relatively to the Impost.*

[See TABLE, N° VI.]

THE impost is a portion of our property, which has ever been, and ever will remain, appropriated and engaged to secure to us the peaceable enjoyment of the rest.

IT is, indeed, possible that a nation should pay no tribute to its government; but it must then pay a tribute to its neighbours, by a political dependance upon them.

SUCH of our lands as are noble, and were formerly salique lands, boast an immemorial immunity from imposts. However, tho' military service, to which the possession of them obliged their owners, so far from being considered as a burthen, was deemed an honour; it was, after all, a subvention: and the possessors

ſeſſors of thoſe lands, whoſe fancied immunity ſound policy will ever reſpect, are by birth, what, in other countries, men are aukwardly deſigned by the red collar; I mean, ſubjects devoted to the ſervice of the public.

IN a word, the impoſt is a debt by the law of nature, that is to ſay, by the law of God and man, provided we give the word *impoſt* its true meaning, and underſtand by it ſecurity and relief, and by no means general oppreſſion.

IT is to no purpoſe to object, that it is doing nothing, merely to indicate the point where words change their meaning, ſince all earthly diſputes ariſe merely from the contrary ſignifications annexed to the ſame expreſſions. Beſides, I might eaſily and with truth anſwer, that hiſtory affords very few, if any, examples of any tribute having ever occaſioned any conſiderable murmurs, when the people themſelves were charged with the collecting of it, and were permitted to bring the produce of it directly to the ſovereign; but we have here a much

much ſurer guide than experience itſelf; for the table will direct our enquiries on this head, even better than it has done on any of the preceeding. Let us firſt ſpeak of the collection of the impoſt; we ſhall afterwards ſpeak of its diſtribution.

A WELL regulated impoſt, that is to ſay, an impoſt which does not degenerate into *ſpoliation* by a bad method of laying it on, is to be conſidered as a portion of the net produce of the lands of a landed nation. Otherwiſe, it would have no proportional rule, either with itſelf, or with the ſaid net produce, or with the condition of the ſubjects liable to pay it; it might inſenſibly ruin every thing, even before thoſe, who laid it on, dreamed of any miſchief.

THIS tribute, therefore, called impoſt, ſhould bear, intirely and directly, on the income, that is, on the annual and well known net produce of the land; and not on the farmer's advances, nor on the labouring people, nor on the ſale of commodities; for in theſe laſt caſes it would prove utterly deſtructive.

IT has been already demonſtrated, by the aberrations of the table belonging to the ſecond and third ſections of the ſecond part, that, when it bears on the farmer's advances, it, from an impoſt, becomes a ſpoliation, that would infallibly put a ſtop to reproduction; impoveriſh the lands; ruin the farmers, the land-owners, and the ſtate.

LAID upon the working part of the nation, and on the ſale of commodities, it becomes arbitrary; the expences of levying it amount to more than the thing itſelf, and recoil without meaſure upon the annual incomes of the land, to the loſs of the ſtate, and of individuals. But we muſt here diſtinguiſh between *impoſition* and *impoſt*. The impoſition would become treble the impoſt, and would bear heavy even upon the impoſt itſelf; for in all the expences of the ſtate, the taxes laid upon commodities would be paid by the impoſt. Thus, then, would the impoſt become deceitful and deſtructive.

ANY impoſt upon the working part of the nation, who live upon their wages, is

no

no better, ſtrictly ſpeaking, than an impoſt upon labour paid by thoſe who employ the labourers; as an impoſt upon horſes made uſe of in tillage, is no better than an impoſt on the very expences of cultivation.

THUS any impoſt upon men, and not on the net produce of the land, would bear upon the very expences requiſite to carry on the different branches of manufactures and agriculture, would doubly affect the ſaid net produce, and quickly annihilate the impoſt itſelf. We are to conſider this impoſt in the ſame light with taxes upon commodities, which likewiſe affect the net produce of land, the impoſt, and the expences of cultivation; and the levying of which cannot fail of being attended with immenſe expences in a great ſtate.

PETTY maritime ſtates, however, which have nothing but their trade to depend upon, are obliged to have recourſe to this kind of impoſt, though in a leſs onerous form. Great ſtates, too, muſt make uſe of it, when their agriculture is ſo decayed, that the net produce of their lands can no longer afford a ſufficient impoſt.

BUT then, ſuch a reſource in ſuch ſtates, is no better than a ſurcharge, which obliges the common people to live poorer than they otherwiſe would, ſtops labour, extinguiſhes reproduction, and completes the ruin of both ſovereign and ſubject.

IT has been often propoſed, that the impoſt ſhould be, like the tithe, levied in kind, by taking a certain part of the crop, or groſs produce of the land; but it would then bear no certain proportion to the net produce; the poorer the land, and the poorer the crop, the more unjuſt and burthenſome would ſuch an impoſt be.

LET us now proceed to the diſtribution of the impoſt, and the eſtimation of its amount, being the points, to illuſtrate which I conſtructed the Table at the head of this ſection. I have, no doubt, grounded this Table on a mere hypotheſis; but the realization of this hypotheſis is ever to be dreaded, ever to be carefully avoided.

I SUP-

I SUPPOSE a kingdom, in which the impost is, in an arbitrary manner, laid chiefly upon farmers, on labouring people, on merchandize, especially those of the remote provinces; that is to say, in which it bears, directly and indirectly, on the advances of cultivation. Let the amount, assumed for basis, be ten millions sterling, ordinary impost, half immediately laid upon the land, and the other half upon goods. I suppose, on the other hand, that the charges of levying it amount to as much more.

Now, the immediate net produce of the lands of this nation would, in process of time, amount to no more, to judge of it by a scrutiny into the tax of one tenth on the productive funds, and into the total produce, than about twenty millions sterling, including tithes and other ecclesiastical revenues, nay, and the very impost payable by these revenues; a dismal produce for so large and so fertile a kingdom, and so laborious and numerous a people.

As, in general, great evils attend capital errors in the administration of the

 finances,

finances, we muſt likewiſe ſuppoſe, that in this country the taille is arbitrarily impoſed upon the huſbandman; that the exportation of corn is forbid; that the production is limited to the conſumption of the nation; that half the lands lie fallow; that the planting of vines in places fit for them, is prohibited; that wines are overburthened with ruinous impoſitions; that the domeſtic trade of corn is ſubjected to an arbitrary police; that even the tranſportation of it from one province to another, is liable to perpetual interruptions; and that the venal value of commodities is continually fluctuating.

IN conſequence of ſuch a ſeries of deſtructive meaſures, the ill adminiſtred impoſt muſt fall heavy on the huſbandman's advances, to the prejudice of reproduction, which would then, of courſe, decay from year to year. The huſbandman's children would abandon the country; the extraordinary weight of the impoſt, on the natural price of commodities, and on workmen's wages, would raiſe both one third on the proprietary claſs,

claſs, ſo as to reduce their twenty millions ſterling, in point of real value, to leſs than thirteen millions and a half; and prove of equal prejudice to foreign commerce, and the employment of the impoſt remaining in circulation.

AN impoſt upon wages and commodities cannot fail being attended with a heavy expence of adminiſtration and collection. Beſides weakening circulation, and reſtraining commerce, it raiſes the price of wages and commodities to the amount of the whole produce of the impoſt; that is to ſay, if an impoſt on conſumption brings in 1,250,000*l.* and coſts an equal ſum to levy it, the goods, upon which it is raiſed, muſt coſt the conſumers 2,500,000*l.* more than they otherwiſe would do. Now, as the general maſs of the impoſt muſt be expended, the impoſt itſelf muſt likewiſe immediately loſe one third, ſince it pays for every thing one third, or even more, than it would do without that impoſt, which it really pays itſelf to the collectors and managers of it; ſo that from 10,000,000*l.* it is reduced to about 6,700,000*l.*

LET us now suppose, that there are, in the state, general farms let out, for example, at 5,000,000*l.* and the levying of 5,000,00*l.* (including the general farmer's profits) costs 10,000,000*l.* Let us then examine this formidable, and, in the general opinion, so important operation of farming, by the foregoing reduction; it will appear that this impost of 5,000,000*l.* immediately lessens the public revenue of the state by 3,300,000*l.* How so? Because this operation draws after it the 10,000,000*l.* charges of perception, and those 10,000,000*l.* form a bastard addition to the venal value of commodities. Now, as the exchequer is the great steward and caterer of the state, it pays the 3,300,000*l.* above-mentioned, for the share of these 10,000,000*l.* Hence it follows, that this is no better than taking with one hand, to give with the other; that this admired farm of 5,000,000*l.* sinks in real value to 1,650,000*l.* and nevertheless costs those who contribute to it 10,000,000*l.* extraordinary, in charges of administration and perception, and in profits to the *persons employed against the king*.

BUT

BUT a ſtill worſe effect of this fatal method would be, as the Table demonſtrates, that of hindering annually the reproduction of more than 6,700,000*l.* for the ſake of an impoſt, that would ſink to 1,650,000 *l.* and which it would be an eaſy matter to raiſe otherwiſe, tho' it amounted to the 5,000,000*l.* promiſed by the farms, ſo as to ſave the nation upwards of 10,000,000 *l.* in the expences of perception, beſides the above 6,700,000 *l.* annually deſtroyed by the method of farming.

SUCH is the unavoidable miſchief of impoſts upon goods, not to ſpeak of the enormous prejudice they do to commerce. Thus, then, it appears, that this kind of impoſt does not deſerve the name of impoſt; it is no better than a depredation, which ruins the ſubject, without doing any ſervice to the ſovereign.

THIS deceitful and deſtructive impoſt would, beſides, give a falſe idea of the annual net produce of the lands, and other riches of the kingdom. On the one hand, people would

would be apt to make this net produce amount to about 20,000,000 *l.* never ſo much as dreaming that both it, and the whole of the impoſt, reduced to their real value, would form, in the whole, but about 20,000,000 *l.* On the other hand, they would make the impoſt amount to 20,000,000 *l.* which, in the whole, would look like a total net produce of 40,000,000 *l.* but, in ſpite of this confuſion, it muſt clearly appear, that the land-owner's income of 20,000,000 *l.* and the total impoſt of 20,000,000 *l.* which, in appearance, form a net produce of 40,000,000 *l.* form, in fact, but a net produce of 20,000,000 *l.* and that the ſurpluſage of 20,000,000 *l.* conſiſting entirely of baſtard impoſts, and baſtard charges, is no better than an excreſſence of barren and burthenſome expences. By adding to this proſpect, the loſſes cauſed by the detention of money in the coffers of ſaving people, and in the uſurpous trade of the financiers, it will appear, that all altogether, every year, radically leſſen the net produce by about 27,500,000 *l.* ſo as to reduce the advances of the huſbandman, the

net

net produce of real eſtates, the value of lands, the labour of the hands employed in manufactures, and the impoſt itſelf; not to mention the progreſſive decay which ſpoliation draws after it, occaſioned by that part of the arbitrary impoſt laid upon the farmers, which, added to the want of a market, cauſes lands to fall into petty culture, or lie entirely uncultivated.

THIS was once the caſe, and when it was, the expences of cultivation produced no more, including the impoſt, than 20 or 25 *per cent.* and that they produced ſo much, was owing to the great cultivation, which ſtill exiſted in one fourth of the kingdom. We do not calculate in what number of years this degradation muſt happen, becauſe the different deſtructive cauſes, of which we have ſpoken, may contribute to it more or leſs, as they act jointly or ſeparately. We ſet out at a point of degradation, which we are well acquainted with. Conſult the article CORN, in the *Encyclopædia*, where you will find in what manner a nation may loſe annually four fifths of the net produce

produce of its huſbandry. Thus the general maſs of riches, which, while agriculture flouriſhed in the nation, might amount to 4,000 or 4,500 millions, would appear reduced to 900 or 1,000 millions.

THE beginning of this degradation is referred to the year 1690, or thereabouts. It would be an eaſy matter, by purſuing the ſame order of declenſion, to calculate how long it may ſtill hold; but arithmetical truths of this kind are too deciſive, and too harſh to let us puſh our enquiries ſo far. We ſhall not, therefore, follow the rapid progreſs of this declenſion; it may be eaſily gueſſed by the expoſition we have given of it in the Table, and as eaſily ſtopped before it utterly ruins the ſtate.

IT is very mortifying to be thus obliged to deſcend from ideas of infinity, and give up the flattering ſuppoſitions of the inexhauſtible reſources of a great kingdom, eſpecially at a time, when a greedy or ambitious heart ſeconded, in this reſpect, the illuſions of the mind; but it is ſtill more mortifying to be undeceived by real facts, and ſee oneſelf, at

the

the end of a long courſe of falſe œconomy, and ſecret depredations, after half an age of miſtaken parſimony, during which, men of the greateſt fortunes were reproached with an expenſiveneſs, that men of middling fortunes might formerly have allowed themſelves; during which a ſpirit of plunder prevailed every where, becauſe a ſpirit of taxing ſpared nothing; it is much more mortifying, I ſay, to find one's ſelf, all at once, in a ſtate of abſolute exhauſtion, as if heaven and earth were hardened into braſs, and all in conſequence of a ſingle miſtake, but that indeed a fundamental miſtake, from which all the reſt naturally follow. A great kingdom, like *Anteus*, in the Table, muſt fall into agonies, as ſoon as its communication with the earth is cut off. It is from the earth alone, that ſuch a kingdom can draw all its forces, and it is upon the earth alone, that it can recover them.

THE author of the Detail of *France*, under *Lewis* XIV. printed in 1699, refers, as we have already ſaid, the beginning of the declenſion of the kingdom to the year 1660. He

He examines the progreſs of it to the time he publiſhed his work, and demonſtrates, that the net produce of our lands, which in 1660 amounted to 35,000,000*l.* (equal to 70,000,000*l.* of our money at this day) had ſunk one half by the year 1699. He takes notice, that it is not to the quantity of the impoſt, but to the bad choice of objects it was laid on, and to the diſorders which then attended the levying it, that this enormous degradation muſt be attributed. We are to judge of the further progreſs of this diminution by the continuation of the ſame kind of adminiſtration. The impoſition, at length, became ſo exorbitant, that under *Lewis* XIV. it amounted to upwards of 37,500,000 *l.** which brought into the king's coffers but 12,500,000*l.* ſo that the contributors were annually robbed of 25,000,000 *l.* the reproduction of 10,000,000 *l.* of which was, beſides, every year, irretrievably loſt. Theſe diſorders, likewiſe, annually preyed upon the ſtock of national riches to the ſame amount; and, including the annual deſtruction occaſioned by the

* Memoirs for the general hiſtory of the finances, by Monſieur *Deon de Beaumont.*

the arbitrary taille laid upon the farmers, the whole formed an annual depredation of more than 15,000,000*l*. Thus, then, the depredation amounted every three years to about 50,000,000*l*. (nearly equal to 100,000,000*l*. of our money at this day.) This ruinous impoſition, which bore heavy on the expence of the impoſt itſelf, reduced it, in point of real value, to about 8,500,000 *l*. and, after all, I mean nothing here, but what, in matters of finance, is called groſs impoſt; that is, ſuch impoſt as has not yet ſuffered by paſſing through the hands of the receivers and treaſurers; who may be compared to ſo many uſeleſs inns, where the public money pays dearly for its reception. Accordingly, it has been obſerved, that both prince and people may be greatly enriched, even in ſo ſhort a time as a month, by a better adminiſtration, that would aboliſh ſo ruinous an impoſition, revive the exportation of corn, wine, wool, linnen, *&c.* But the man, who ſhould dare undertake ſuch a reformation at a time when all right notions concerning the œconomical government of an extenſive kingdom were loſt, would have been

been accuſed of an attempt to overthrow the pillars of the whole edifice.

HAVING thus diſcovered the ſource of the evil, calculated the progreſs of it, and demonſtrated the Table, it may now, perhaps, be time to point out the remedy.

IT appears, in general, that the impoſt ſhould be levied directly on the net produce of the earth, ſince, in whatever manner it is levied in a kingdom which draws its riches from its territory, it is always ultimately paid by the land. Thus, then, the ſimpleſt and moſt regular form of impoſition, the moſt profitable to the ſovereign, and leaſt burthenſome to the ſubject, is that which is immediately, and with due proportion, laid at the ſource of the continually renaſcent riches.

WE are told, that a flouriſhing nation, though burthened with ſubſidies on a great number of commodities, and confined to a territory of no great extent, has, nevertheleſs, found means to confirm her power, and ſecure

ſecure its proſperity, by exempting the plough from every kind of burthen. The farmers pay no impoſt: the land-owners who do are liable, no doubt, in time of war, to tranſitory ſubventions, which, during the ſtorm, may oblige them to leſſen their expences; but, then, huſbandry goes on as uſual, and the ſale and venal value of the immediate fruits of the earth are held up by the freedom of exportation. Agriculture, and the multiplication of cattle, ſuffer nothing by the longeſt, and moſt expenſive wars. The land-owners find their lands, at the return of peace, well cultivated, and in good heart; and their rents as good, and as well paid, as ever.

BY this we may eaſily judge of the difference between an exorbitant impoſt, and a ſpoliative impoſt; for, according to the form of laying it on, an impoſt may be ſpoliative without being exorbitant, and exorbitant without being ſpoliative. This appears in the caſe of *England*, which, inexhauſtible in conſequence of her ever renaſcent riches, is thereby enabled to maintain the moſt obſtinate wars by ſea and land, without the leaſt loſs or diminution of her forces.

IT appears, however, by what we can gather concerning the public revenues of this nation, that however wiſe and patriotic her government may be, they are very far from proceeding on this occaſion upon true and ſimple principles. Accordingly, we ſee her over head and ears in debt: but then her attention to avoid ſpoliative or deſtructive taxes, and never farm her revenues *, ſecures her from fundamental ruin, notwithſtanding the great abuſe ſhe makes of her ſtrength, and the miſtakes inſeparable from exorbitant deſigns, and too diſtant enterpriſes.

DURST I now, after pointing out what is to be avoided, ſay what is to be done, it would, with whatever juſtneſs combined, be ſufficient matter for a ſeparate work, being the reſult of an infinite number of enquiries, and compariſons.

* I am informed, that, by an ancient law, the bare propoſal of a farm or monopoly is felony in *England*, and puniſhable with death.

IT is no eaſy matter to adjuſt a tax upon lands, ſince they are to be rated, not only according to what the fee of them is worth, but likewiſe according to their relative value. Middling lands, near a good market, are often worth more than the beſt at a diſtance from one, ſince the venal value is every thing. Now, from market to market, we, at laſt, reach the interior markets, maritime commerce, the open ſeas, *&c.* It is thus that all the branches of œconomical harmony correſpond with, and depend upon, each other.

THE difference, which different modes of culture occaſion in the produce of the earth, is ſufficiently manifeſt from the foregoing pages; and likewiſe, that there is a mode of culture made uſe of in certain exhauſted nations, which ſcarcely yields any produce. It likewiſe appears, that it is not enough to teach, and to recommend a better kind of culture, conſidering the heavy charges requiſite to eſtabliſh it. No, the hands of the huſbandman muſt be ſtrengthened; it is only the ſtrength of them, that can make the earth yield her produce, as it is only this produce, that can ſupply the exchequer. The exchequer, however, as the lungs of a political body, ſhould never ſtand ſtill, but be continually drawing in, and throwing out riches. But how can riches be drawn from products which never exiſt?

FROM all this it follows, that the cadaſters *, repreſented elſewhere, as an almoſt indiſpenſable baſis of regeneration, afford, conſidering the injuſtice and abſurdity of the arbitrary perſonal tax upon the huſbandman, a very unequal and burthenſome form of repartition, which makes no allowances for great calamities equally unforeſeen, and unavoidable. We muſt, therefore, think of ſome more juſt, more ſimple, more paternal plan, and find out ſome method of winding up the machine, ſo as to make it go of itſelf with little or no expence; and likewiſe make the revenues of the prince conſtantly keep pace with thoſe of the people, in order to bind and unite for ever, what ought never to have been ſeparated. We muſt endeavour to cure people of the notion, that, to ruin themſelves, and

* Regiſters, containing an account of the nature and value of the lands of every diſtrict.

and waſte their patrimony, is the way to thrive, and to conquer. We are now . . . . But it is not yet time. One word more, and we might expect to ſee our works placed among thoſe called *the reveries of a good ſubject*. We muſt uſe great gentleneſs in addreſſing nations frivolous enough to make a god of that idle ſcarecrow, called *Ridicule*, which, however, does infinite miſchief, ſince, *as long as all the world is in the wrong, all the world is in the right*. Tho' I am thus ſuddenly ſtopt ſhort by the fear of being ridiculed for being righteous over-much, I have often defied other kinds of ridicule. But this kind would render me hereafter uſeleſs to my country.

CONCLUSION.

BY recollecting ſucceſſively all the truths eſtabliſhed in the different applications of the Table, and referring them in this place to the article upon the impoſt, it will eaſily be ſeen,

1ſt, THAT every penny attending the perception of impoſts, is ſo much transferred to the barren claſs; an enormous diſorder this in the table!

2d, WHAT expences of the ſtate are ruinous in their own nature; what likewiſe are a means of accelerating circulation; and what, in fine, are advantageous, by flowing almoſt entirely into the productive claſs.

3d, IN what manner the bare miſapplication of uſeful expences may render them ruinous. For example, regular troops, maintained with the produce of the nation, ſtrengthen the productive claſs; whereas, ſent abroad, they become ruinous to her, though foreigners were to maintain them, merely in conſe-

consequence of her losing the benefit of their consumption.

4th, THAT those, who are always preaching up to their sovereign a dry and barren œconomy, are unacquainted with the first principles of true political œconomy. The government of a nation, blessed with a fruitful and extensive territory, should consume a great deal, to make the country produce a great deal; but then the country must not be plundered, because there can be no thief without a receiver, and there should be no receivers to lock up any thing in a flourishing state. The state, I say, must consume a great deal. But to consume a great deal, it must have a great deal to consume; and to have a great deal to consume, the subjects must be rich; the lands must be in full production; the advances of agriculture and manufactures, the husbandman and the manufacturer themselves, all kinds of commodities, the markets, &c. must be entirely exempt from all burthens. The whole of the impost must fall upon the net produce of the earth; pass directly without any round-abouts from the purſes of the ſubject into the coffers of the ſovereign; and, in the diſburſement of it, from the coffers of the ſovereign, into the purſes of the ſubjects. But this is the grand ſtumbling-block in the way of all attempts to bring about a reformation: 'tis here the beſt miniſters meet with obſtacles ſuperior to all their courage and virtue.

SUCH, however, was the project of *Sully*, which *Henry* IV. tired with ſeeing his pot empty, and all his doublets worn out at the elbows, laid before his council of finances. But they unanimouſly anſwered, that it was the project of a mad-man, who thought that the revenues of a great ſtate were to be governed like thoſe of a private family; to which this prince, no leſs judicious than frank and open, immediately replied, that *they, who were ſuch wiſe men, having ruined him, he had a mind to ſee if mad-men could not make him whole again.*

RECAPITULATION.

IT is, in a manner, impoſſible to give any abſtract of a work, that is in itſelf but an abſtract of demonſtrations and principles, which handled, as fully as they ought to be, would alone be ſufficient to fill volumes. All I can do, then, is to give a kind of index, that may juſt point out the principal object of every ſection of this development.

The author, before he exhibits his table, acquaints us with the object of it, ventures to invite the learned to apply themſelves, as to the performance of a duty incumbent on ſuch ſubjects, to the ſtudy of the œconomical ſcience. He then warns us of the difficulties which attend his elements, and gives a preparatory ſketch of the ſimple manner of entering this career by the road which his table exhibits.

Next comes the explanation in two parts. The firſt, ſub-divided into ſeven ſections, acquaints us with the nature of the table. The

The ſecond, in an equal number of ſections, preſents us with the development and conſequences of it.

FIRST PART.

SECTION I.

The OECONOMICAL TABLE *conſidered in its Conſtruction.*

THIS table is no more than a map of circulation, and takes in nothing but the land-owner's ſhare of the net produce of the land, excluſive of tithes and impoſt, ariſing from a vigorous cultivation, that yields one hundred per cent. net on the annual advances required by it, beſides ten per cent. on theſe and the primitive advances. This ſhare of the land-owner is equally divided, and goes one half to the productive, and the other half to the manufacturing claſs.

THIS ſection gives the firſt explanation of this new kind of dialect, and aſcertains the natural and neceſſary produce of an acre of corn-land in a vigorous ſtate of culture, free and exempt from all manner of taxes, and rendered

rendered valuable by an advantageous foreign commerce, ſecuring their juſt venal value to the immediate fruits of the earth.

SECTION II.

The OECONOMICAL TABLE *conſidered in its Progreſs.*

THE table is the ſame here as in the preceeding ſection.

HERE we ſee circulation going forward; we ſee the diſtribution of money, which, though in itſelf no more than a conventional riches, is the indiſpenſable attendant of real riches; we ſee where every portion of real riches ſhould tend, and where it ſhould ſtop; where be conſumed, and where reproduced; and what are the advantageous effects of the mutual ebbing and flowing of the productive and barren claſſes one into the other, which in reality doubles riches, and in appearance trebles the effects of them, by means of an extenſive, rapid, and equal circulation.

SECTION

SECTION III.

The OECONOMICAL TABLE *considered relatively to Populousness.*

NO alteration as yet in the table. The Author establishes, in the simple language of calculation, the true principles of population, a population secured to the state by the strongest of all ties, the ties of subsistence. He here pretty nearly points out, what must be the relative number of adults to the other inhabitants in an agricole state; what portion of these adults may be disposed of, and applied to such employments as are not of absolute necessity; likewise, what portion is indispensably tied down to the different purposes of production and manufacture. Hence flows the grand and genuine principle of population, namely, that a state, which would encrease the number of its subjects, can do it only in proportion as it increases the quantity of its riches. This demonstration, afforded by a bare survey of the Table, which proves that riches can spring from nothing but production, brings back population to its radical principle, *agriculture.*

SECTION

SECTION IV.

The OECONOMICAL TABLE *considered relatively to the Amount of the Impost and Tithes.*

HERE the Table attains its full growth, by the addition of one half, and of one quarter of what the land-owner's share of the net produce of the land amounts to; the first appropriated to pay the king his tribute, and the second to pay the church her tithes. This is the only alteration in the Table, for the whole amount of these three portions of the income combined together is here supposed to circulate in the same order with the rent alone in the preceeding Tables.

I SET out by shewing, that these contributions, so profitable both to the sovereign and the subject, are, yet, no way exorbitant, and that the proprietary, and every other class, would be extremely happy, that things were established upon this footing.

SECTION

SECTION V.

The OECONOMICAL TABLE *considered relatively to the National Cash.*

THIS is a repetition of the preceeding Table. This section is intended to direct our ideas concerning money, in which all the riches of a state is, by vulgar opinion, made to consist; and demonstrates, that, as it is impossible to establish any fixed notion on this head, it is equally useless to investigate the quantity of money in a nation, since it must ever be in proportion to the annual net produce of her lands; and that all the money besides, hoarded up by avarice, is rather an incumbrance than an advantage to the state. The circulating cash of a nation can only be in proportion to the amount of her other riches.

SECTION VI.

The OECONOMICAL TABLE *considered in the Estimation of the Produce, and of the capital Stock of every Kind of Riches.*

THE Table is still the same. The estimate contained in this section is nothing less than ideal, since the main assertions of of it are built upon inconteſtable principles already eſtabliſhed. Nor are the moveable riches rated too high in proportion to the net produce of the lands, comparatively at leaſt with what we every day experience this way. Beſides it is always of ſervice to be able to make an eſtimate of one's condition. This valuation was moreover neceſſary to point out the real rank and dignity of money, an object ſo enormouſly magnified in the imaginations of moſt people.

SECTION VII.

The OECONOMICAL TABLE *conſidered in the Conditions neceſſary to the free Play and Proſperity of the political Machine.*

THE preceeding Table is here again repeated. This is a kind of recapitulation of the conditions neceſſary to a free, full, and perfect circulation, ſuch as is cauſed by a vigorous and plentiful production; and a caution againſt all the falſe meaſures that may obſtruct it. I cannot too earneſtly recommend a careful peruſal of this kind of repertory, which takes in a great

great many objects, and omits few of those which belong to this so extensive and practical a science.

SECOND PART.

AFTER letting the reader into the nature of the Table, in the preceeding part, we present him with the development of it in the second part, by exhibiting the consequences of any disorder that may creep into it.

SECTION I.

The OECONOMICAL TABLE *considered in its private Depredations, Excess of Luxury, &c.*

THE Table is here presented in its first disorder, proceeding from a distribution of one sixth more of the annual net produce to the barren than to the productive class. The failure occasioned thereby very naturally appears at the bottom of the Table, by following the rules laid down for that purpose.

IN this section, after taking a cursory view of some of the principal causes of the ballance of of the table inclining to the barren claſs; we aſcertain in what conſiſts the proſperity of a landed nation; we anſwer ſome ſpecious arguments in favour of petty cultivation; and return to the ſupport of our concluſive demonſtrations, that great advances are requiſite to ſecure every kind of rural profit.

SECTION II.

The OECONOMICAL TABLE *conſidered relatively to a State of Spoliation.*

THE Table here appears in the ſtate of fifty livres diminution on one thouſand and fifty, conſidered as the capital of the annual advances of the productive claſs.

THE detail of the depredations ſets out with the firſt objects that occur, the effects of which are not abſolutely capital and peremptory. Here is ſhewn, how the manners and cuſtoms of a nation affect it in its phyſical capacity. After which, as we go on, we treat of thoſe devaſtations which go to the quick, and which in a few years wear away to nothing all the riches of a ſtate. This is what we call *ſpoliation*, that is to ſay, the deſtruction of the advances neceſſary to cultivate the

 earth

earth to advantage. We here ſuppoſe, that the ſpoliation takes annually fifty livres from the farmer's annual advances of one thouſand and fifty livres; we ſhew, what the deficiency is the firſt year; the rapidity of its progreſs; and how quickly it muſt end in an abſolute and entire devaſtation; for ſuch is the unavoidable conſequence of it. This ſpeculation, at length, ſhews us, how agriculture declines to ſuch a pitch, as to yield no longer above twenty per cent net on the advances of cultivation, inſtead of one hundred per cent. which it yielded, at firſt, in its natural ſtate of proſperity.

SECTION III.

The OECONOMICAL TABLE, *in which the Decay of Huſbandry, and the ſad Effects thereof relatively to Population, are conſidered.*

WE here exhibit the table in that ſtate of net produce, which we have been juſt ſpeaking of, that is to ſay, yielding no more than twenty per cent. of the annual advances.

WE demonſtrate, in the explanation, the conſequences of ſuch a decay, and bring back the

the ſtate of population to its true principles, namely, its proportion with the earnings, profits, and ſalaries of the ſeveral branches of the ſtate. We likewiſe curſorily examine, in what conſiſts a ſtrong and numerous defence; armies being nothing elſe than a diſpoſeable or ſupernumerary portion of the inhabitants, whoſe ſtrength and maintenance are ſubject to the ſame rules with the ſtrength and maintenance of the other portions. We here alſo point out the uſeful way of employing the ſupernumerary hands in public works, the expence of which proves advantageous to the nation, in regard to her commerce, her commodities, &c. and ought to fall to the ſhare of the ſeveral provinces, in proportion to their contributions, and be directed by them ſeverally, as parties principally concerned, though in conformity with the general views and deciſions of the government.

SECTION IV.

The OECONOMICAL TABLE *conſidered in its Diſorders relatively to Money.*

THE foregoing Table ſtill lies before us.

WE

We here put the reader in mind, that money is but an intermediate pledge between buyers and ſellers; and that the money in a landed nation can ſcarcely exceed the annual net produce of her lands; that money cannot indemnify for any deficiency in the ſucceſſive renewals of riches; that the ſcraping together of money ſhould not be the object of a nation's paſſion; that money can never be ſcarce in a well cultivated kingdom; that when a nation ceaſes to have any produce, it is impoſſible ſhe ſhould retain her money.

Section V.

The Oeconomical Table *conſidered in its Diſorders relatively to the Police.*

THE ſame Table ſtill lies before us.

We here conſider the moral cauſes of the decay of the Table; we particularly dwell upon the miſchiefs proceeding from prohibitions too commonly conſidered as the effects of a ſound police.

SECTION VI.

The OECONOMICAL TABLE *considered in its Depredations relatively to Commerce.*

THE Table ſtill continues on the footing of twenty per cent. net produce upon the annual advances.

DEFINITION of commerce; its effects; its advantages when free from errors. Sketch of the illuſions in commercial matters of a great prince, and a great miniſter. The works of the manufacturer no ſource of riches. The profits of maſter manufacturers, and merchants, often no better than burthens with reſpect to the nation. That importation of wrought commodities, which favours the exportation of unwrought commodities, very advantageous to a landed nation.

SECTION VII.

The OECONOMICAL TABLE *conſidered in its Depredations relatively to the Impoſt.*

HERE the Table aſſumes a new aſpect, being conſtructed on the footing of a real net produce of four hundred livres, and a burthenſome impoſition to the amount of four hundred livres more, too often taken for

net

net produce, both forming a total of eight hundred livres, of which two hundred livres, half of the real net produce, paſs over to the productive claſs, and ſix hundred livres, viz. the remaining two hundred of the real net produce, and the other four hundred, conſiſting of baſtard impoſts, and burthenſome impoſitions, paſs over to the claſs of barren expences.

THIS diſorder ariſes from the quality and ſpecies of the impoſition. This is made out in the laſt ſection. A reaſonable impoſt ought to be conſidered as a portion of the net produce of the land taken from it without any manner of expence or depredation. Tribute can come from nothing but the ſaid net produce. Devaſtation of a ſtate, in which the impoſt ſhould be arbitrarily laid upon the huſbandman, the manufacturer, proviſions, or merchandize. How the impoſt preys upon itſelf, and loſes, by encreaſing the price of every thing it is iſſued to purchaſe, double of what it gains by the encreaſe of its receipts. How the impoſitions, that is to ſay, the charges of collecting the impoſt, double the above diſadvantage, ſo as entirely to abſorb itſelf. How, in conſequence of theſe

two

two errors, the revenues of the ſtate, and thoſe of the land-owners, come to have but an empty amount, and a fictitious value, the two parts of which, in fact, run into each other, and form, in reality, but one poor heap of ruins, comparatively with what might be expected in an extenſive and fertile kingdom.

HERE the friend of mankind finiſhes his career; here he takes his leave of the ſervice in which he had dedicated himſelf to his prince, to his fellow-ſubjects, to mankind. His hairs begin to look grey; he has ſeen the meridian of life, and the public ſhould not be made to bear the decline of it. In his firſt work, he gave a plan of paſtoral adminiſtration; in the ſecond, he treated of the principles of organization, and the manner of realizing its details as to the municipal part; in the third, in fine, he points out the qualities of riches, and the means of procuring them; he frees the firſt notions from the prejudices, reduced into principles, with which ignorance and paſſion had ſurrounded and ſtifled them. This triple development forms a ſketch of the whole of political œconomy. Such was, ſuch ought to have been, the uſe of his voice; at leaſt ſuch he intended it ſhould have been. He will deem himſelf happy, if his cotemporaries or poſterity reap any advantage from his labours! Nay, he is happy in having undertaken them with that view. In his progreſs

greſs he has oppoſed two authors, but not two men, for he knows them not; and if he did, it would be as a brother to their perſons, though an enemy to their principles. Were he to meet them, the rencounter could not be as warm, as was his firſt converſation with him who affirmed, that he had not hit upon one true principle of population. He withdrew, as people generally do from all diſputes, as much as ever of his own opinion; but he recovered of himſelf; he liſtened again; he ſtudied; and he has ſince had reaſon to thank himſelf for doing ſo. He did homage to truth, and from truth he has received ample returns for his homage. But had he found in the man, that oppoſed him, a tool of the finance, a compiler of oppreſſive ordonances, he would never have quitted the field, till he had blaſted his opinions. This he is not afraid to ſay he has often done, and will be ever ready to do again on the firſt alarm.

All to this he has finiſhed his career, his glaſs is run. Let the man, whom he has perſonally offended, ſtand up and accuſe him; but if that man is not to be found, he hopes that all in general will condeſcend to receive his laſt adieus in the ſame manner they beſtowed their welcomes on his firſt appearance.

FINIS.